Just Call Me Jane

Just Call Me Jane

Dennis Solon

Copyright © 2013 by Dennis Solon.

Library of Congress Control Number: 2013914744
ISBN: Hardcover 978-1-4836-8426-0
Softcover 978-1-4836-8425-3
Ebook 978-1-4836-8427-7

All rights reserved. No part of this book may be reproduced or transmitted in any form or by any means, electronic or mechanical, including photocopying, recording, or by any information storage and retrieval system, without permission in writing from the copyright owner.

This book was printed in the United States of America.

Rev. date: 09/06/2013

To order additional copies of this book, contact:
Xlibris LLC
1-888-795-4274
www.Xlibris.com
Orders@Xlibris.com
140350

Contents

Acknowledgments 9

1. Christmas Morning 11
2. The Life Of Jane 17
3. Jane Has A Baby 21
4. Moving In With Grandpa And Grandma 24
5. Jane's Breakdown 29
6. Jane Goes To Work 31
7. Our Wedding 36
8. The Weekend Everything Changed 43
9. Jane's First Christmas Visit 49
10. Jane Moves To Troy 52
11. Moving West 62
12. Ohio Christmas Stories 64
13. Jane Moves To Dayton 71
14. Jane's Surgery 76

This book is dedicated to

My wife, Martha Solon,

And our four children,

Mark, Michael, John, and Shannon

Acknowledgments

I have always had people who knew my mother tell me that "someday someone should write a book about that woman." While I sometimes had the inclination to write her story, I never seemed to find the time. However, I was forced to have a spinal fusion and the recovery period meant months away from my golf game. I now had the time to write my mother's story, which turned out to be my story as well.

Because this would be a totally new venture for me, I was looking for help and input from many directions.

Undoubtedly, Martha, my wife, was my biggest helper and supporter. I want to thank her for putting up with Jane and her bizarre ways all those years. Martha also has a degree in English, which came in very handy when editing the book.

Next I would like to acknowledge our four children, Mark, Michael, John, and Shannon. They all had to deal with Jane. They reminded me of some of Jane's eccentricities which are mentioned in this book. Most of all, I want the kids to know that I sincerely regret that Jane was not a better Grandma to them. Grandmas are wonderful people and our kids missed out on that joy in life.

I appreciate the input of Rosie Browning, our friend and accomplished teacher of English, who read the first draft and made many suggestions that I welcomed and incorporated into the book. I would also like to thank Sandi Faber for her contribution and editing skills.

Many thanks to Dee Domingo, our neighbor and computer guru. I could not have put this book on a flash drive without her.

I would be remiss if I did not acknowledge all of my friends who gave me such positive encouragement. My friend Jeanie Williamson suggested the title, and Nancy Campbell, my former secretary, shared some of her memories with me.

Every story about Jane in this book is true and is written exactly as remembered by folks who dealt with her directly. To my brother-in-law Jerome Carrigan, my nephew Jay Carrigan and his wife Lisa, my niece Michele, and certainly John Nelson, I just want to say "thanks for remembering."

Chapter One

CHRISTMAS MORNING

As young kids growing up, Christmas was always a very special occasion for both my wife Martha and me. We each reminisced about celebrating Christmases with our respective families. As children we had both experienced the anticipation of visits to department store Santas, the magical window displays, the aroma of Christmas cookies being baked, midnight masses, and opening presents with our families on Christmas morning. When we started our family, we knew that we wanted our Christmases to be just as special as the ones we recollected from our childhoods. We wanted our children to remember Christmas as special, an event that would be meaningful not only in a religious way, but also as a time of family festivities. This Christmas was to be no exception, at least that's what we thought.

The time was Christmas morning 1987. We usually attended mass on Christmas eve, so Christmas morning was a time when our family would customarily relax and exchange our gifts. Martha and I and two of our children John, 21, and Shannon, 18, were seated in our living room in Fort Myers, Florida, along with Aunt Cass. Cass, 78, was one of my father's older sisters. Since Cass's husband Uncle Clarence had passed away several years earlier, Martha and I would drive over to Boynton Beach and bring Aunt Cass over to the west coast to spend Christmas with us so she would not be alone for the holiday. Our oldest son Mark was with his wife Clare celebrating Christmas in Canada with her family. Our second son Mike was in Dayton, Ohio. Mike was a student at Wright State University, and when we moved to Florida in 1984, he remained in Dayton to continue his schooling. This particular Christmas he decided to spend in Dayton with his girlfriend Chris and her family.

Several weeks before Christmas we received a strange Christmas card from Mike. No kidding . . . the front of the card read "Guess who is coming for Christmas?" When the page was turned, it read "Not me." Now Martha and I thought that was a really strange card, and we wondered if we were not wasting our money sending this boy to college, but, oh well, that's the way kids can be sometimes. We thought nothing more of the incident and Christmas morning was pretty typical as we began settling in the living room to open our gifts. As usual, Shannon handed out the packages.

Our family was never one to put too much thought into presents, so the gifts were nice, but nothing too unusual. Everyone was opening their gifts, which consisted of an assortment of cardigan sweaters, golf outfits, pajamas, and cologne. About half way through the ritual, Shannon picked out a rather large box which had been sent by Mike. She did the honors of opening the box and pulled out a present for her, one for her brother John, one marked for Mom, and last, but not least, was a present that Shannon handed to me marked "Dad," along with a note that said, "Dear Dad, I thought you would like to spend one more Christmas with Grandma."

Now, Grandma was Jane, my mother. I handed the mysterious note to Martha, who was sitting beside me. She looked puzzled as she read the note, but said nothing. I began stripping the paper off the parcel, uncovering a heavy plastic bag the size of a large thermos bottle. The yellow descriptive tag on the bag read, "George Miller and Sons Funeral Home." When Martha spotted the plastic bag and tag, she immediately grabbed it from me and dashed into the kitchen. From where I was sitting in the living room, I could see that she was not acting normally. She was frantically motioning for me to come into the kitchen! I abruptly left the family gathering and rushed in to see what was bothering Martha. She was completely silent, with a stricken look on her face, pointing to the plastic bag that Mike had sent to me. I took a good look at the parcel and realized that our son, who wasn't spending Christmas with us, had sent me my mother's ashes as a Christmas gift. I was taken aback, but at the same time, I was so proud of his sense of humor that I actually chuckled. That kid is funny, just like his dad. A moment later a thought flashed through my mind: "What the hell am I going to do with Jane's ashes?" I couldn't figure it out when she died, and I sure didn't have any answers at this moment. Poor Martha was in utter shock. She quickly stashed the parcel in our utility room, hoping that Cass had not noticed the minor commotion. If she knew that we had Jane's ashes, she would stroke out on the couch! We already had one body to deal with, so to speak.

Jane had died from complications of heart and lung problems on December 11, 1980, when Martha and I and our four children lived in Dayton, Ohio. Jane also lived in Dayton, only six blocks from us at the time. Living near my mom was more of a curse than a blessing, which I will explain later. Then you will understand my unusual actions at the time of her death.

Let's get back to 1987, Christmas passed; we drove Cass back to Boynton Beach, the kids started school, Martha returned to her teaching job, and I was busy trying to fill my sales quota. I moved Jane's ashes from the utility room to the shelf in my office, but I faced that same old dilemma that I had failed to deal with in 1982 when Jane died: What the hell to do with Jane's ashes?

I confided in my Florida friends. Once they recovered from the shock of knowing that I still possessed my mom's ashes seven years after her death, several people recommended that I send the ashes to my father's grave in Hammond, Indiana. I could have his grave opened and put her ashes in with him. "After all," they said, "they had been married for twenty-three years, and perhaps it would be nice if they were joined together in death." Let me tell you that being married to Jane for years was not what I would describe as ideal. When it came to love and affection, Jane just didn't have it in her to demonstrate those emotions. She never showed any real affection towards my dad. When my father was sick and in the hospital, Jane would always inquire about Paul's condition, but never showed any real affection towards him. So each time people would suggest opening Paul's grave to join them in death, I would quickly respond, "Are you insane? Paul went to his grave trying to get away from her and her treacherous ways. There is no way I would ever do that to my dad!" So, for the time being Jane remained on a shelf in my home office closet, hidden from constant view. Jane's ashes had now been with us nearly a month.

Martha has a birthday in January, and so does my brother-in-law Jerome. In fact, their birthdays are only one day apart. Ever since we moved to Florida, one of our traditions was for Martha's sister Mary and her husband Jerome to travel from Illinois to our house in Florida in January for a week's vacation. When they arrived this particular January, one of the first things we told them was how Mike had mailed Jane's ashes to me as a Christmas gift. They thought it was outrageously funny that Mike would do such a thing! They could not stop laughing, since they had known Jane and were very aware of her crazy escapades and the hell she had put us through for some fifteen years or so. Mike's prank caused outbursts of laughter from Mary and Jerome on several occasions that week.

The week's vacation went well. We all enjoyed the beach, eating out, and lots of shopping and sightseeing. But as normal, all good things must come to an end, and so it was with this vacation. Mary and Jerome were packed. Their suitcases were on the bed in the guest room and they were busy saying good byes to Martha and the kids, and just reminiscing. I began reflecting about how amusing they thought it was that Mike had mailed Jane's ashes to me. As I pondered the thought, I realized that Jane never really got a chance to travel. So this seemed to be a perfect opportunity for her to take a trip. At that point, I lifted Jane down off the office shelf and hid her in Mary's suitcase. It wasn't long before it was time to head for the airport. Hugs and kisses and a normal farewell and they were off for St. Louis.

On the way home from the airport, I mentioned to Martha that Grandma was gone. She looked at me in total amazement. Of course, she wanted to know where she had gone. I explained how Grandma had found her way into Aunt Mary's suitcase, and she was high above Florida on her way to St. Louis. At first she was dumfounded; then she started to think about the situation and she couldn't stop laughing. "You know," she said, "they will be calling us the minute they get home and start unpacking."

It was 11:30 p.m. in Florida and 10:30 p.m. in Godfrey, Illinois, when our phone began ringing. Mary was not quite sure what to say or do and Jerome was yelling, "You son of a bitch, you crazy son of a bitch," but he was also laughing. My nephew Jay and his new wife Lisa had picked up Jerome and Mary at the airport. They were in the background and also in a kind of shock. My understanding was that Lisa was running down the hall, waving her hands in the air, yelling, and wondering what kind of a family she had married into.

Mary asked, "What am I going to do with Jane?"

I thought for a minute and responded, "Aren't your brothers Gib and Jerry stopping over tomorrow night before flying out to California to visit Aunt Blanche?"

"Yes," Mary said.

"Well, put Jane in Uncle Gib's suitcase. She has never been to California."

We called Mary the next evening, but she hadn't sent Jane on the plane with Gib and Jerry. I guess Jane wasn't meant to go to California.

Months passed, and in the course of a phone conversation one evening, I asked Mary and Jerome if they had ever done anything with Jane's ashes. "Yes," they told me. They had gone out on their boat on Alton Lake (the Mississippi River), and they had sprinkled Jane's ashes, along with some flower petals, on the water, said a prayer, and more or less gave Jane a proper burial. I was not sure if they telling me a story, or if that is what they had really done. However, there was really no way to prove anything one way or the other.

Later that summer I had a class reunion in Illinois, so Martha and I decided to take a road trip up to Kankakee, my home town. On the way up, we decided to stop in Godfrey and visit Mary and Jerome. I always doubted that they had really poured Jane's ashes in the river, so one day when Jerome was at work, I went down in the basement and snooped everywhere to see if I could find Jane. I found not a single trace of her, and therefore, I was pretty sure they had poured her in the river. I told Martha when we left for Kankakee that I never found Jane, so I was certain it was as they had said.

Several years passed, and Mary and Jerome would come for a visit every January. Nothing was really ever mentioned about Jane's ashes. Once in a while, something would come up about some of the things she had done and the problems she caused, but nothing about her ashes. It was a forgotten issue.

One Saturday morning in June, I was playing golf with some friends. Charlie and Al and I often played in the 8:00 o'clock shotgun, and this week we were joined by my friend John. Our foursome started on the 14th hole. When we came around to the number one hole, I felt a few drops of rain. I had complained for some time that my golf bag felt heavy, and when I purchased it, I thought it was a light-weight bag. I decided to retrieve my rain suit from the large storage compartment on the back of the bag. As the sprinkles continued, I unzipped the opening and was reaching for my rain suit when I felt a plastic bag the shape of a large thermos bottle. I knew at once what it was: my mother's ashes. Sometime on one of my brother-in-law's visits to Florida, Jerome had transported my mother's ashes back to Florida and put them in my golf bag. My best guess is that Jane had been in my golf bag for over a year. I pulled out the plastic bag of ashes along with my rain suit and hopped in the driver's side of the golf cart and set the bag of ashes on the floor.

My friend John immediately asked, "What the hell is that?"

I responded in a matter-of-fact tone, "It's my mother's ashes. My brother-in-law put her in my golf bag."

John was speechless, but finally managed to sputter, "What are you going to do with them?"

I thought for a moment, and then I said, "The only thing she ever really liked was golf." I took a golf tee out of my pocket, ripped open the bag, and spread her ashes on the golf course.

Now John was really in shock. He said, "Did you just do what I thought you did?"

"Yes," I said. "I finally laid my mother to rest." I offered him the opportunity to say a prayer.

In his shock, he declined the opportunity, saying, "You are the coldest son of a bitch I ever met."

At that point we headed for the green. The first thing John did was tell Charlie and Al what I had done.

He asked, "Could that have really happened, or is it all some sort of a joke?"

Charlie and Al both said that they knew Jane had done some traveling, but they didn't realize that she had come back to rest in my golf bag. So, yes, it really was possible. John's game was shot for the day. At that point I promised him that some day I would tell him the whole story and, "John, I guess this is the day."

Chapter Two

The Life of Jane

This is the life story of Jane Bick, born Jane Louise Bick on March 31, 1915, to Peter H. Bick and Mary Elizabeth Bick, formerly Mary Elizabeth Kiley. Pete's family emigrated from Germany in the 1880's and settled in the Chicago area, where Pete met Mary Elizabeth Kiley. They married and settled in Hammond, Indiana. Pete and Mame, as they were known, were to become my Grandpa and Grandma. Pete started a real estate and insurance business which prospered and afforded Grandpa and Grandma a comfortable living. They started a family—four daughters, each spaced two years apart. The oldest was Mary Katherine, known as Mary K. The second was Elizabeth, followed by Anne, and the last was Jane Louise, my mom.

When I was growing up and visiting my parents' friends in Hammond, I was made aware of some idiosyncrasies that my Grandma Mame possessed. At the time I was told these stories, they were quite amusing, but much later in my life I realized that the patterns set by Grandma had long-term effects. I was told, "You know your grandma really only had one daughter—that was Mary Katherine. Grandma never developed a real mother-daughter relationship with the other three daughters. Because of this favoritism, the other girls always resented Mary K. Later in life, they referred to her as "mother superior" because she was always very bossy. She was the only daughter to attend college. She attended Saint Mary of the Woods Catholic College, an elite girls' school in Terre Haute, Indiana. I never knew if Mary K. was the only one to go to college because of favoritism or because of the economic change that befell the family. The stock market crash and Great Depression were totally devastating to Grandpa's real estate and insurance business. Mary K. had to drop out of school, but she remained in the area, never married, and ultimately became administrator of the James O. Parramore Tuberculosis Hospital. She remained in close touch with her mother and father, returning home on weekends.

The second daughter was Elizabeth. Liz, as she was called, was the black sheep of the girls. Liz never seemed happy. The girls would tell all kinds of stories about Liz. She had a quick temper and was not beyond chasing her sisters with a butcher knife in hand, threatening to kill them if she could catch them. As a child, she would steal from her sisters or do whatever she thought she could get away with. She apparently was like this as an adult as well.

One day, many years after the daughters were grown, Mary K. received her Marshall Fields credit card bill, only to discover over one thousand dollars in charges she knew nothing about. After investigating, it was discovered that Liz, who Mary K. had not seen in years, had forged Mary Katherine's signature on sales slips. I suppose she had retained her penchant for larceny. Mary K. fortunately was able to straighten out the situation and did not have to pay the $1000 bill.

On another day, while shopping in Marshall Fields, Mary K. had another encounter with her wayward sister. Mary K. was on the ground floor of Marshall Fields looking at some leather gloves she planned to purchase. She glanced up and there stood Liz. Mind you, she had not seen her in over twenty years.

"Liz," she said with a gasp.

Liz looked up, spied Mary K., and dashed out of the store, leaving Mary K. standing and staring after her.

Mary K. never saw or heard from her sister again, not even when their parents died.

Unlike Liz, Anne was the easy going, soft-spoken daughter. She always seemed to get along with her sisters. After graduating from high school she went into nurses training and eventually practiced nursing at Saint Margaret's Hospital in Hammond. She married a doctor named Allen Shackelford. Allen was drafted into World War Two, and made the service his career. Anne and Allen traveled and lived all over the world. Ann, like Liz, never returned home, even when Grandma and Grandpa passed away.

Jane was the youngest daughter. There is no doubt that Jane resented the favoritism shown toward "mother superior." Long after they were adults, Jane referred bitterly to Mary K. as "mother superior" and "her royal highness." Surely as a child she must have felt slighted when she could not capture her mother's attention and affection. However, she did find approval somewhere in the family. Her father, my grandpa, was very creative, and he and Jane would plant flowers in the yard in the spring, and Jane would assist him when he decorated the house for Christmas. She and her father developed a very close bond. When Jane graduated from high school, she immediately went to work in her dad's real estate and insurance office. She was good with numbers and had great organizational skills. She was a real natural in the business world. Having the opportunity to watch her father building, buying and selling real estate was a great training ground. It wasn't long before Jane developed a real entrepreneurial side to her personality. The business struggled because of the Depression, but Jane continued working for her father and enjoyed the challenges of business and the close relationship she had with him. Her father was the parent whose approval Jane enjoyed. One can only imagine Jane's devastation when she was told, several years later, that her father was bisexual, and everyone knew it with the exception of her family.

In the early spring of 1937, Jane met Paul Solon. Their courtship lasted about six months before they became engaged. They were married at St. Joseph Catholic Church in Hammond, Indiana, on September 25, 1937. The happy couple took a short honeymoon to Niagara Falls. After returning to Hammond, they moved into the Cordova apartment building on Ruth Street and started their married life. Jane went back to work with her dad and Paul resumed his job as an electrician for the Indiana Harbor Belt Railroad.

Paul Solon, Joseph Solon and Jane Solon

Paul and Jane Solon on their Wedding Day!

Chapter Three

Jane Has A Baby

In 1941, the USA entered WWII. Paul was not drafted because of his job on the railroad. The railroads were a primary method of transporting supplies and troops. Anyone who worked a job that was critical to keep trains running was not eligible for the draft. Paul worked for the railroads for over twenty three years before he was forced to take an early retirement for disability reasons.

When Jane and Paul decided to move from the Cordova apartments, they moved to 254 Locust Street. There were two identical four unit apartment buildings on Locust Street. These two buildings were right next door to each other, but the amazing thing was that these apartments were in the middle of a very nice single-family-home neighborhood. Jane and Paul moved into unit C which was on the second floor across from apartment D. The apartment was approximately 900 square feet. It consisted of a living room, one bedroom, one bathroom, a dining area and kitchen.

On August 10, 1940, I was born. I have been told many times that once I came home from the hospital, Jane's organizational skills and her attention to detail became her main focus. Not just the baby, but everyone around the baby was on schedule. There were certain times for naps, and, believe me, no one got to visit or play with the baby if it was nap time. Meals were also on a schedule as well as play time. My meals were very well thought out for nutritional value before anyone really paid attention to things like nutrition. Jane was happy and content to take care of her baby, clean, and prepare meals. Motherhood agreed with her.

When I was young, Jane and Paul were both very good parents. I never wanted for love and affection. Jane always would prepare a nice evening meal, and when Paul got home from work we had dinner together. Evenings were Paul's time to spend with me. The older I got, the more activities we enjoyed. As a youngster, I spent loads of time outside. Since the neighborhood had a lot of families, there were always kids to play with and things to do. When Paul got home, we would play whatever sport was in season: football in the fall, baseball in the spring and summer, and sledding and snowball fights in the winter. We didn't have a very big yard, but it always seemed to work for whatever game we were playing. The only down side of the neighborhood was at the end of our street was the Monon Railroad switching yards. All the kids were warned to stay away from the trains and the railroad yard because of the danger. We were also cautioned about the hobos that rode the trains. These men were very scary to little kids, so no one ever went around the train yards. However, if we did and got caught, we were in for the whipping of our lives.

There were very few kids who grew up in Hammond between 1940-1950 who didn't know Doctor Clancy. Doctor Clancy was our local pediatrician, and Jane thought he could walk on water when it came to taking care of kids. If I ever looked sick or if she thought I may have been exposed to something, we were on our way to see Doctor Clancy. Diseases such as mumps, chicken pox and measles were a threat that concerned all mothers, but of course the big fear was polio. I guess sometimes Jane was overly cautious. However, whatever the problem or whatever the ailment, Doctor Clancy always came to the rescue and Jane felt a sense of relief.

Then came the day that our world started to change. I was in third grade when Jane received a phone call from Paul's work. Paul had been taken to Saint Margaret's Hospital by ambulance because he was suffering with severe chest pains. Jane went to the hospital and sent someone to come across the street to Saint Joseph grade school to bring me over to the hospital. Paul was 34 years old and had never really been sick, so his chest pains puzzled the doctors. They could not believe that someone so young could be having a heart attack.

After a few anxious days, the doctors attributed Paul's condition to indigestion and released him. I believe my dad was told to take a few days off and rest. The doctors could not really find anything that made them think that Paul had heart trouble. They started running a lot of tests and went out of their way to prove he could not have had a heart attack.

Paul returned to work, and for a short time things went back to normal. The doctors advised Paul to quit smoking and change his diet, but Paul was a meat and potatoes person. He didn't like vegetables or dairy products of any kind, and salad was never a part of his diet. Jane did her best to help him make changes in his life style, but she did not set a very good example by smoking two packs of Camels every day.

Over a period of time, my dad continued to have periods of chest pains and shortness of breath. On these occasions, he would be rushed to St. Margaret's Hospital. I can remember many times sitting in my classroom at Saint Joseph's. I would hear the ambulance going past to the emergency room, and I would watch the classroom door to see if someone would be coming to take me to the hospital because my dad had had another attack.

Some days Paul would have as many as four separate attacks in the same day. He was starting to have to miss work because the doctors wanted him to rest. In those days, that was the treatment for heart disease and stress, but they still were not convinced that my dad had heart trouble.

While all this was going on with my dad, Grandpa and Grandpa were approaching their mid to late seventies and their health was also failing. Jane's world really started to spin out of control. How could she manage caring for a husband with serious medical problems, tending to two parents who were ailing, and continue her duties as a mother?

The time soon came when the family had to make some changes that would make life a little more manageable for Jane. It was ultimately decided that we would move from 254 Locust Street to Grandma and Grandpa's house. Finances were a problem because Grandpa didn't have any income since the real estate and insurance agency had long since closed, and Paul's income was cut because he wasn't working. Aunt Mary K. said if Jane would take care of Grandpa and Grandma, she would pay a substantial part of the bills. She had a very good job in Crown Point and very few expenses and that was a way she could contribute to Grandpa and Grandma's well-being. She also planned on coming to Hammond on the weekends to help Jane with their parents. It was the best arrangement that could be made. Mary K. would help pay the bills, and Jane would be mom, nurse, and housekeeper.

Chapter Four

Moving In With Grandpa and Grandma

Grandpa and Grandma lived at 24 Elizabeth Street. They had lived there for more than twenty years. Grandpa actually built the building in the late 1920's when the real estate business was successful. They originally lived next door and Grandpa built 24 Elizabeth St. as an investment. However, when the Depression started, he sold the house they were living in, and he and Grandma moved to 24 Elizabeth St. The house was a two-story structure with one apartment on each floor. The building had a large glass front door. That door led to a spacious entry way with two doors. The door on the left went to the upstairs apartment and the one on the right went to Grandpa and Grandma's, where we now lived. The door led directly in to a formal parlor with French doors that led into the living room. Straight ahead was a large brick fireplace with bookcases on each side. To the right was a nice sitting area with a large bay window. From this area one could see up and down the street in both directions. From the parlor doors looking left, there was a long hallway. The first door to the right was the master bedroom and to the left was a large dining room. The dining room had a large oak oval-shaped dining table that could easily seat twelve people. Moving on down the hall, the next doorway on the right led towards both the bathroom and a walkway that led back to the master bedroom. The kitchen was on the left side of the hallway. The kitchen was large, and on one side was a breakfast room, which was converted into my bedroom. On the other side was a large pantry area. Across the hall from the kitchen was a good size bedroom that was Grandpa's bedroom and at the end of the hall there was another bedroom on the right that was Grandma's bedroom. At the end of the hall was a door which led to the enclosed back porch.

When we first moved in to Elizabeth St. things went along really well. I was nine years old and able to walk to school; Paul was working on a regular basis, and everyone's health seemed good. Jane and Paul were able to go out on Saturday evening for dinner, and they didn't have to worry about someone staying with me because Grandma and Grandpa were there, and most of the time Aunt Mary K. would come home for the weekend. However, this didn't last very long. My dad started to have more attacks and was continuously being rushed to St. Margaret's Hospital. That meant Jane had to be at the hospital, so who was going to fix dinner and do all the other chores at home? Paul had so many of the attacks, as they called them, the doctors finally told him that they wanted him to go to Rochester, Minnesota, to the Mayo Clinic. They believed that is where the best doctors were and they had the latest equipment. So Jane and Paul flew to the Mayo Clinic. After several days and many tests, the doctors concluded that Paul had an advanced case of coronary artery disease. This was very unusual for someone in midlife. Paul was only 34 years old at the time and appeared to be in good physical condition.

When Jane and Paul returned from the Mayo Clinic, it seems like our life really took a change and certainly not for the better. At the same time Paul was attempting to quit smoking, Jane was trying to change his meat and potatoes diet to something much healthier like salad, chicken, and fish, grilled, not fried. Paul was unwilling to change. He never quit smoking. He didn't quit the meat and potatoes either.

The entire time Jane was trying to help Paul with his lifestyle changes, she had to deal with Grandma and Grandpa. Not only were they getting older, they were not pleased with the diet changes or having a nine-year-old living in the house, bouncing a basketball around in the kitchen. I guess it would be fair to say that tensions in the house were running pretty high most of the time. Who knows, maybe this is what caused Grandma and Grandpa's health to go downhill. Someone was always in the hospital.

I was an altar boy from second grade all through grade school, and on Sunday, I would go to Saint Margaret's Hospital to serve 6:00 a.m. mass with Father Schmidt. The reason I mentioned this is because I always remembered that after mass I would always have to go and visit either Dad, Grandma, or Grandpa. It just seemed like one of them was always in the hospital, and if they were not in the hospital, they were at home in bed. So Jane not only had to try to raise her young son, but she was constantly dealing with three people who were close to her who were in various stages of poor health. Jane functioned like a programmed robot, showing no real emotion. She just dealt with each day as it came along. There was no escaping.

In July of 1949, Jane started to feel sick. She was nauseated a lot and just felt totally run down. She finally decided to tell our family doctor, Dr. Robert Husted, who was a personal friend. He decided to run some basic tests, and much to everyone's surprise, Jane was pregnant. I can't remember how long the morning sickness lasted, but, based on her schedule, Jane could not afford the time to get sick. Too many people were relying on her on a day-to-day basis.

To the best of my knowledge, Jane's pregnancy was pretty normal. I remember that when she started to show, she would take my hand and hold it on her stomach so I could feel the baby move. Now for a ten-year-old boy that was a really exciting feeling. I don't remember what Grandma or Grandpa thought about Jane being pregnant; I am sure they thought it was fine. However, I do remember very well how excited Dad was about having another child. It was all he could talk about. I guess it was the first positive thing to happen in their lives in a long, long time. He would ask me if I would rather have a little brother or a little sister. I really don't remember having a preference. Knowing myself as I do, I probably wasn't looking for any competition. I just remember that I thought the whole idea was pretty special, and everyone seemed to be in a contented mood.

Jane and Paul would sit around and read names out of a name book, and they would always ask me what I thought about this or that name. I really do not remember many of the options that were considered, but I do remember that having a new baby became a bigger focus than a house full of medical problems.

Well, as time went on Jane got bigger and bigger, and everyone was getting more excited about the new baby. Would it be a boy or a girl? I don't remember what name was decided on for a boy, but if the baby was a girl, then her name would be Janet.

As the pregnancy progressed, so did Dad's heart problems. He would work for a few weeks, then suddenly he would be rushed to Saint Margaret's Hospital because he was having more heart attacks. I remember the episodes like they were yesterday. I would be at school and hear the ambulances arriving at St. Margaret's. It wouldn't be very long and one of the nuns from the hospital would be knocking on my class room door. Sister would go to the door and the two nuns would talk in the hall for a second. Then Sister would call me out in the hall, and the nuns would tell me that my dad was in the hospital, and I needed to go with Sister because my dad was "Real bad and he wanted to see me." I remember on the way back over to the hospital Sister told me, "Dennie, your dad has had several heart attacks today. He probably will not live through the night."

When we would get to his room, I was usually afraid to go in because I was afraid he was going to die. When I did enter his room, I saw that the head of his bed was covered with a large plastic oxygen tent. Paul would always hold out his hand from under the sheets so I could hold it. He spoke only in whispers because of the oxygen tent. He was very weak, so it was hard to understand him. He had the nurse hang my picture on the wall in front of his bed so he could see it. As I remember, this photo was about a 5x7 that I guess Jane brought from home. After I had visited for a while, Jane would have someone pick me up to take me home. When I got home, I remember placing one of the kitchen chairs by my bedroom window. I would kneel in the chair, look up to heaven, and pray that my dad would live through the night. I guess God always listened to me because he always seemed to make it.

The real test of Dad's heart came on March 27, 1950. Paul had had one of his episodes, so was not working and was home resting. I had gone to school that morning and everything seemed normal. When I came home from school, Paul was sitting on a love seat in the bay window in the front part of the living room. He was crying. He composed himself enough to tell me that Jane had to go to the hospital because something was wrong with the baby. The umbilical cord had wrapped around the baby's neck, and the baby had died. As I sat next to him on the love seat, he put his arm around me, and we both sat there crying for a long time.

I had never experienced anyone I was close to dying, and I just knew that it really hurt. Dad said that the baby was a girl. He told me that Jane was going to be okay, and she would be home from the hospital in a couple of days. Then my aunt Cass came over. She had been at the hospital with Jane because Paul could not go. I will never forget what Cass said to me when she came in the room.

She looked at me and said, "She looked just like you."

I just stood there, not knowing what to say. I went back to my bedroom and lay down. The baby was taken to Cavalry Cemetery where she was buried with my dad's mother, her Grandma Solon. When Jane came home, she seemed fine, and things seemed to go back to normal or what was normal for our house. She was back to caring for her parents and looking after my dad and me like nothing ever happened.

Paul was 36 years old and fairly strong, but his heart was in real bad shape. The doctors said that there was a new type of open heart surgery and because of his age and his overall strength, they felt Paul was a strong candidate for the surgery. They also felt that he really didn't have any other options; his heart would last only six months without the surgery. Of course, there was no other choice; Paul would have open heart surgery as soon as possible.

In late January, Paul was taken to Michael Reese Hospital in Chicago because that is where Doctor Emanuel Marcus practiced. He was the surgeon who had been trained to perform this new open heart surgery. The scheduled date for the surgery was February 2, 1952. I believe it was one of the first times this surgery had been performed in the United States. Paul's operation took over 6 hours and ultimately it was considered a success, but his hospital stay lasted for over 3 months.

So here was Jane with her husband in a hospital fifty miles away in Chicago, her parents at home in poor health, and a young son who needed his mother. Through all this Jane remained in control, but also a bit distant. I never saw her cry, and I do not recollect her ever putting her arm around me or asking me how I was doing. If I asked how my dad was doing, she would tell me he was going to be just fine and that was it.

After what seemed like an eternity, my Dad came home and started his long road to recovery. He had already been hospitalized for three months, and he was not able to work for at least three to four more months. He had all types of special diets to contend with. At that time, the doctors didn't know much about rehabilitation, so he was told to sit around the house and rest until his doctors gave the okay to start back to work. Even going back to work was on a limited basis, maybe three half days a week. While Paul seemed to be doing much better, Jane was finally starting to succumb to the constant stress.

Chapter Five

Jane's Breakdown

In 1953, Jane had a nervous breakdown. It may have resulted from all the stress in her life. In today's world, she would likely be treated for depression. Medicine has made large improvements in the last fifty years, and there are now many new drugs that are used to help people suffering from depression. Let's go back sixty-two years. The most common treatment used to treat a person in a state of depression or suffering from a nervous breakdown was to use electric shock treatments. The patient would be fully conscious. He or she would be placed on a table, in some cases strapped down or held down by the orderlies or nurses. A metal band would be positioned around the head, and a rubber tongue depressor placed in the mouth so the patient could not bite off her tongue while the electricity was administered. Electrodes were then placed on the patient's head, and finally the doctors would administer the electric shock. The body would shake violently. This was the barbaric treatment used on Jane during her stay at Wise Memorial Hospital. I do not know how frequently Jane was subjected to these treatments, but I do know that her stay at Wise Memorial Hospital lasted for about two and one-half to three months. Jane was released from the hospital in time to come home for my eighth grade graduation from Saint Joseph School. When Paul brought her in the house, I was shocked. She didn't even look like my mom. She looked completely different from the way she had looked when she left for the hospital. She appeared very frail and weak. Her thick brown hair had turned completely gray. I remember wondering what had happened to my mom.

It wasn't long after graduation that Paul announced that the railroad was transferring him to Kankakee, Illinois, a town located about fifty miles southwest of Hammond. Kankakee was a prosperous small city of about forty-five thousand people with a lot of light industry, such as Roper Stove Company and A. O. Smith Water Heaters. We had always lived in Hammond, so this was a big move for the whole family. The question then became: who will be taking care of Grandma and Grandpa? After some deliberation, Aunt Mary K. and Jane determined that Grandma Mame would move with us to Kankakee, and Grandpa Pete would be moved to a nursing home. Pete and Mame had been married for approximately 45 years and now they were going to be separated.

Moving day arrived. Grandpa insisted that he was not going anywhere. He was going to stay in his house. When the moving van pulled away, Grandpa was left with a living room chair, a lamp, some kitchen furniture, and a bed, in a nearly vacant house all by himself. I had lived in this house with my grandpa for the last five years, and now, as we were driving away, I wondered if I would ever see him again. I never did. He stayed in that house alone for three nights before a cousin took him to a nursing home. I do not believe Jane ever went to see her father. He passed away five years later while I was in college.

Chapter Six

Jane Goes To Work

We had never lived in a single family home. We had always been in apartments. Dad was back to work and doing everything he could to create a positive environment for Jane to improve. As time went on, we became more of a normal family. Paul was doing well physically and working; I was a freshman at East Jr. High School playing sports and making friends. It wasn't long before Jane started looking for a job and was hired by two doctors to manage their new office.

Times were good for about four years while I was in high school. Jane was secure in her job. The doctors liked her, and she enjoyed running the office. Paul's job went well. Jane and Paul had become friends with the neighbors and started to have a social life playing cards with the neighbors, cooking out on the charcoal grill, and dining out on Saturdays. About the time I graduated from high school, Dad was having some heart-related problems, and it became apparent that he was going to have to take an early disability retirement.

Dad was only about forty-four years old, and he did not want to just sit in a chair and wait to die. He decided to go back to school to train as an investment broker. Every morning he would catch the Illinois Central train to Chicago where he was in class all day, then return home to Kankakee on the evening train. He would arrive around 7:30 p.m., have dinner, and then study for a couple of hours. He provided me with a great role model of the importance of studying and improving oneself. Eventually he graduated from investment school, but the big test was still to come. He had to pass the Illinois and Indiana state license examinations. He passed them both on the first try. He was then hired by a brokerage firm named Waddell and Reed, and he would be selling a new product called mutual funds.

Jane continued to do well with her job, but Grandma was getting feeble and she was no longer able to be left alone all day. Jane and Paul moved her into a nursing home very close to the office where Jane worked so she could easily stop by and visit her mother each day. The move was good for Grandma because she was not home alone and she had people to talk to every day.

Jane really enjoyed her job. She proved herself as a competent office manager, and Dr. Lang and Dr. Urlich recognized that she had a good head for business, so they approached her one day with a proposition. Kankakee did not have a hospital supply business. It was a community of approximately 45,000 thousand and the two adjacent counties, Will and Iroquois, were economically dependent on Kankakee. At that time, everyone had to order hospital supplies from Chicago and the turnaround time was slow. Dr. Lang and Dr. Urlich proposed opening a local hospital supply business that would be operated by Jane. They would provide the financing, and Jane and Dad could pay them back out of the profits. Jane immediately recognized this as a great opportunity. She came home and told Dad she had something she wanted to discuss with him. She explained the doctors' proposition.

Dad listened intently and then he responded. "We don't know anything about running a business, and besides I would never borrow money from anyone, especially an amount that large." He questioned how the money could ever be repaid. Paul simply did not envision himself in the role of a businessman.

This was no doubt a missed opportunity and probably a great frustration for Jane.

In 1958, I graduated from Kankakee High School and left for Carbondale, Illinois, to attend Southern Illinois University. I met a girl named Martha, and we dated for about five months before the end of my freshman year. I went back to Kankakee for the summer where I worked on the railroad. Before I knew it, fall was here and I was returning to Carbondale to begin my sophomore year at SIU. Dad was doing well at Waddell and Reed, and Jane was busy with her work at the doctors' office and visiting Grandma at the nursing home. Dad would occasionally drive down to Carbondale and visit Martha and me (we were now a serious couple). Whenever I would visit my folks in Kankakee, Martha was there with me. Dad really enjoyed Martha's visits. He was very affectionate, and he and Martha immediately bonded. It was like she was the daughter he had lost ten years before. Jane was much more reserved, not showing any open affection, but was always courteous towards Martha.

Summer of 1960 meant another stay in Kankakee. I would again be working on the railroad. Martha's mother had died suddenly in January, so Martha planned on spending the summer in her home town of Gillespie, Illinois, with her dad. Dad drove to Carbondale and loaded up things for both Martha and me. Dad and I would give Martha a lift home and then drive on to Kankakee. When we arrived in Gillespie, Martha's dad and my dad had a drink. Martha's dad invited us for dinner, but my dad seemed anxious to get on the road.

I was driving as we headed up Route 66. When I glanced at my dad in the passenger seat, I saw that he had tears in his eyes.

"What's wrong?" I asked.

He then started to explain that when we got home, in the morning, he was planning on leaving Jane. He had been living in Calumet City during the week for about six months because of his work with Waddell and Reed. He now planned on separating from Jane and moving to his apartment in Calumet City full time. He told me that he planned on divorcing my mom, and that she was not aware of his intentions.

I was not surprised with my dad's decision. Some of my aunts and uncles and friends of my parents had told me that they never considered Jane to be a very affectionate or loving wife. Growing up, I had never witnessed my parents showing affection to one another. My dad would speak affectionately to me about Jane, and would sometimes playfully tease her, but she would never join in with the fun. She would remain aloof and indifferent. In fact, she was not above implying that the Solons were not up to the Bick standards. However, no argument would ever erupt.

Although they didn't show affection to one another, they almost never demonstrated anger either. I only recall one incident where Jane lost her temper. It was when I was about ten years old. We lived on Elizabeth Street at the time. Dad and Jane had a huge altercation with Jane screaming and yelling. She even threw a lamp at the bedroom door. I was lying in bed, listening, and had no idea what was wrong. I found out some years later. That was the night my dad told Jane that her father (Pete) was gay, and everyone in Hammond was aware of that fact except Jane and her immediate family.

All of this passed through my mind in the seconds following his announcement, so when my dad asked me what I thought about his leaving, I said, "I would have left her a long time ago."

His first reaction was shock, and his second reaction was anger. "Don't ever let me hear you being disrespectful of your mother," he snapped.

I had told him honestly about my feelings, but he didn't like what he heard. Sometimes you just can't win.

When we arrived in Kankakee, Jane did not seem excited to see me. There were no hugs and kisses or fuss like one would expect from a mother who has not seen her son for several months. I suppose as I got older, she withheld affection from me as well as my dad. The next morning Jane left for work and Paul started to load what was left of his things into his car. Most of his clothes were already in his apartment in Calumet City. Paul wrote a note, sealed it, and left it for Jane. She would find it when she came home from work. As the day went on, I started to realize that my dad was not going to live with us any more, and that I was going to be living with my mom for the summer. When Jane came home, she asked me where Paul was, and I told her he had moved out that morning. I also told her that he had left an envelope for her on the bed in their room. She walked into the bedroom, sat on the bed opened the envelope, and read the note. I watched her and she showed absolutely no emotion. She laid the envelope on the dresser and said, "Let's fix some dinner."

While we were eating dinner, I started to cry.

Jane looked at me and said, "Don't worry; we'll get along just fine without him."

I could not believe her cold reaction to my dad's leaving after twenty-three years of marriage and her lack of concern for her son, who was in a great amount of emotional pain, but this is who Jane had become.

The next morning I took the car and drove the fifty miles or so to Calumet City where my dad was living. He was surprised to see me. I told him I wanted to live with him for the summer. He explained that I had to stay in Kankakee because of my summer job on the railroad.

"Besides," he said, "you have to take care of your mother."

If I remember right, I said something like, "She is your wife, not mine."

At that point he yielded to my wishes, telling me to go back home, and that he would move back for the summer while I was home from school. I agreed and drove back to Kankakee.

That night after work, Jane asked where I had gone. I told her that I had gone to see Dad, and that he agreed to move back for the summer. Once again, she showed no emotion.

Dad moved back that weekend, and things went back to what was normal for 688 Hammes Avenue. I worked on the railroad, Martha visited on weekends when she could, Jane continued to work for the doctors, and Dad continued commuting to Hammond/Calumet City selling mutual funds. The summer passed, and I returned to Southern Illinois University to begin my junior year. Dad moved back to Calumet City permanently. Whether or not he planned to divorce Jane remains a mystery, because he never again spoke of their marital problems.

Chapter Seven

Our Wedding

It was May 13, 1961, a beautiful spring day in Carbondale, Illinois. Martha and I had been together for two and one-half years and wanted to marry. We knew that waiting until after graduation would probably be the prudent decision, but we were young and in love. We could not wait another whole year without living together. We did discuss the idea with Martha's father, but he was against our getting married. He felt that Martha would not complete her final year and graduate. His argument was to no avail. Martha and I decided to marry no matter what. We would marry in Carbondale, a quiet ceremony with just family and close friends. We set a date, May 13, and decided that each of us would break the news to our respective parents.

I called home and luckily my dad answered the phone. I told him that, as he knew, Martha and I had been going together for well over two years and we had decided to marry. My dad was okay with the decision because he loved Martha and thought it was definitely in my best interest to settle down.

Jane's reaction was completely different. She picked up the phone, saying, "What did this girl do to trap you into doing this? Did she tell you she was pregnant? Well, if she did, you have a doctor confirm it before you go through with this marriage."

I finally hung up and figured I would leave the rest to Dad. Perhaps he could handle Jane better than I.

Martha's dad was not overjoyed that his daughter was marrying in her third year of college, but if he wanted this to be a family affair, it was best to go along with our decision. At least his daughter was marrying a good Catholic boy.

The wedding went off as planned. My dad must have done his job convincing Jane, because all the relatives from both sides showed up along with all of our college friends.

Martha and I had rented a two-room furnished apartment on the second floor of a two-story Victorian house. The apartment was spacious, with a kitchen, bathroom, and living room that also contained a double bed! Martha and I had cleaned the place up, arranging things just like we wanted. I actually moved in two weeks before the wedding. I loved the independence and anticipation that Martha would be joining me soon.

When Jane and Dad and my Aunt Cass arrived the day before the wedding, I think Jane was irked that her son would be marrying and living in such humble circumstances, but she said nothing. That afternoon, Dad and I went to the Rasthskeller, a local pub, for a beer and a visit. When we returned a couple of hours later, Jane and Cass had rearranged the entire place. Hmmm. What would Martha think of this?

That evening, Martha's dad arrived, along with her sister Mary and her husband Jerome. Cass and my dad, Martha's family, and our best man, Jerry Eskoff, enjoyed a rehearsal dinner, followed by opening gifts at the new apartment. Jane seemed uncomfortable the entire time, almost frowning, and was coldly cordial to Martha's family. I only observed her becoming animated one time at our apartment that evening, when she was engaged in a conversation with Cass. Jane was very concerned that the expensive silk dress that she had purchased for the wedding might have wrinkled in the suitcase. Would the wrinkles hang out? It would be pure disaster if the dress was rumpled. Her other concern was that people might not realize how expensive her new blue hat was.

"After all," she remarked to Cass, "these people probably would not recognize quality when they see it."

The next day, I did not observe even a hint of a smile during the wedding or the reception that followed. This demeanor persisted the entire weekend, dampening our high spirits. We should have known then that Jane had the ability to put a damper on many events.

It was only three months after the wedding when Martha and I realized that we could not stay in Carbondale and remain in school on the money we were making. We had become really good friends with Sharon and Jim Finley, a young married couple attending SIU. They had moved to Collinsville, their home town, because of better job opportunities and more affordable housing. Since we made so little money, we would qualify as tenants of a nice subsidized housing development located there. Also, SIU had a branch in East Saint Louis, Illinois, about 15 miles away and Saint Louis was just across the river. We could attend SIU, thus living up to our vow to Martha's dad that she would graduate. We relocated, moved into the subsidized housing project of Northgate. Our apartment was just across the parking lot from Sharon and Jim's place. Martha got a job working for the SIU library, and I went to work for the State Bank of Collinsville. On April 30, 1962, our first son Mark was born, just one month before Martha graduated.

As soon as my dad learned of Mark's birth, he was there as fast as the car would travel. He was a proud grandpa and could not wait to see and hold his first grandson. Jane did not come with him and I never understood why. After all, she was a new grandmother. I discovered later that she was not very fond of being a grandma. She said she was too young to be a grandma.

The trip from Kankakee to Collinsville was about five hours, and Paul made it every chance he could. In June, Jane finally showed up when we were going to have Mark baptized. She once again complained about where we lived and our humble circumstances. She and Paul went to a discount store and bought furniture. They came home with a large area rug, a new couch, a chair, two lamps, and two end tables. Martha and I were very grateful to have this furniture and I think Jane was actually pleased. The place looked pretty good.

Mark's baptism was going to be a big occasion. Martha's Uncle Henry would be his godfather and my aunt Mary K. would be his godmother. Martha's family always celebrated holidays and special occasions with family gatherings and this would be no exception. We invited 15 family members for the event.

The day of the baptism arrived. Paul and Jane and Aunt Mary K. represented the Solons. The Ely side consisted of Howard, Uncle Henry, John and Colette and their three children, Mary and Jerome and their two boys. Martha prepared a lunch of chicken ala king and pulled out the good dishes. She was very proud of hosting the whole affair. The baptism went off without a hitch. Once again, Jane didn't smile. I don't think she was too pleased with the cramped quarters and everyone handling the baby.

Once Martha's family left, Jane addressed us and let her opinion be known. The idea of a baptismal party was outrageous. How could we expect to keep a baby on a schedule if we were so distracted entertaining the family? Her lecture must have gotten to Martha, because when our second son Michael was born two years later, we had no celebration whatsoever the day he was baptized. Martha never forgave herself for listening to Jane and cheating everyone out of the joy of Michael's baptism.

That August, Paul drove down from Calumet City to help us celebrate my twenty-second birthday. We really enjoyed having him stay at our place. There was a single bed in the baby's room. He loved holding little Mark, now almost four months old. He would stand at the foot of Mark's crib, watch him sleep, tickle his feet, then tell Martha that the baby was awake. Martha was exasperated, but in a loving way. She knew Paul adored Mark and warned him not to repeat his shenanigans. He reluctantly obeyed. A great relationship was being built. Jane chose not to join us

Jane Solon at Dennis and Martha's wedding day

Jane with Dennis, Martha and Paul

Paul hugging Martha

Paul, Jane and Aunt Cass (Catherine Volkman)

Jane, Martha's dad (Howard Ely) and Paul at Mark's Baptism

Paul playing with Mark at 4-month old

Chapter Eight

The Weekend Everything Changed

Labor Day weekend of 1962 was to be a fun long weekend. Instead of celebrating with her family, Martha and I were returning to Kankakee for the first time with our new son, Mark. We were looking forward to the normal festivities and showing off Mark to all of our old friends. Jane had also not seen Mark since the baptism in June, so she would notice a huge change in him. On Friday night, Martha and I planned to take Jane out to Sully's, a supper club that she and Dad had frequented almost every Friday night when they were together. Dad planned to meet us when he came into town from Calumet City. Jane had set up a babysitter for Mark so we could all go to dinner. We arrived at Sully's around seven and ordered a drink. Jane was in her element. She seemed at ease in the supper club atmosphere, visiting with us and acquaintances in the room, dressed to the "nines" and enjoying her martinis. Forty-five minutes passed and no Dad. Jane became impatient and expressed her frustration about Paul's inconsideration for us. It is "just like him" to "not show up." We ordered dinner, ate, and still no sign of Dad. By now the martinis had a hold on Jane. It was apparent that Dad was not going to appear and Jane had clearly had enough to drink, so we decided to leave. She continued to rant and rave about Dad all the way home. I knew that he must have been held up, because having dinner with Martha and me would mean a lot to him, even if things between him and Jane weren't the best.

We arrived at Jane's apartment on Elm Street, and the first thing I did was give the babysitter a ride home. It only took about ten minutes. When I returned to the apartment, Jane and Martha were discussing the baby. I headed back to the bedroom to change clothes. I expected to hear from my dad any minute. Sure enough, the phone rang. I reached over, picked up the phone, but it wasn't my dad. The person on the other end of the line was my Aunt Marge, my dad's youngest brother Jerry's wife.

She said, "Dennie, I have some really bad news."

"What are you talking about?" I asked.

Marge's voice trembled as she very slowly said, "Your dad just died at Saint Margaret's Hospital."

I was mortified and numb. All I could utter was, "What happened?"

She explained that on Wednesday of that week my Dad did not feel well, so he checked himself in to St Margaret's. He called his brothers, Duane and Jerry, to inform them of his situation. He advised them not to call Jane or me because he didn't want us to worry. He fully expected to be out of the hospital and ready to meet us in Kankakee on Friday night. Duane and Jerry agreed and didn't think much of not calling.

I was standing there listening to the worst news I had ever received, when Jane came into the room. She had heard enough to know that the conversation was about my Dad.

She spouted, "Well, what the hell has he done now?"

I turned to her, the phone still in my hand, and all I could say was, "He's dead."

She collapsed to the floor and started sobbing.

I thanked Aunt Marge for the call and told her that I would call her back in a little while, but I just wanted to take a walk and think. I was not interested in consoling Jane as you would expect in a normal situation, and Jane surely was not going to make any attempt to console me. Looking back, I really do not believe she would know what to do or what to say in order to console someone.

I walked for about an hour or so, then I went back home. Jane was still lying on the floor, not saying or doing anything at that point. She never asked me what happened to my Dad. I called my Aunt Marge back.

This time she explained that she, Jerry, and Duane had been at the hospital visiting Dad that evening and they wanted to call me and give me a heads up about the situation. They didn't want me to worry and they knew that my dad was being released in the morning. Dad insisted that he would explain everything when he got to Kankakee in the morning. When visiting hours were over, Duane, Jerry and Marge left for home. My aunt told me that when they got home, the phone was ringing, and it was the hospital telling them that Paul had just had a massive heart attack and that they needed to get back right away. They turned around and went right back, but it was too late. Paul was gone. It was September 1, 1962, and Paul was forty-eight years old.

Then Aunt Marge explained that his body was being held at the hospital, and that they would be calling me to ask for permission to do an autopsy. Jane was still on the floor and was not in any shape to be involved in any decision-making issues. It was not long before the hospital called to ask for permission to do the autopsy. I asked the doctor who called if they knew what had caused Paul's death. He said there was no question that Paul had suffered an acute coronary thrombosis. I determined that an autopsy was not necessary.

The next step was to call a funeral home. By now Jane had gone to bed and was pretty much passed out. I called Burnes Funeral Home in Hammond where most of our relatives' services were handled. It was around 1:25 a.m. when I called. They said they were waiting for my call, because they had been notified about Dad's passing.

The next morning when I went into the kitchen, Jane was there having coffee and Martha was feeding Mark. I told Jane what had taken place the night before as far as the autopsy decision and the choice of a funeral home. She said that that was okay. She still never said a word to console me and never showed any real emotion. I told her we were going to have to get packed up and go to Hammond. I told her that Martha, Mark and I had been invited to stay with my Uncle Jerry and Aunt Marge and that Jerry and Duane had offered to help me plan the arrangements.

Once again Jane said, "That's okay. You handle it."

It came as no surprise that Jane had not been invited to stay with Marge and Jerry. Jane had burned her bridges with Dad's family many years earlier. She never felt that the Solons were as sophisticated as the Bicks, and she let it be known that when she married a Solon, she had married beneath herself.

When we lived in Hammond, Jane never wanted to visit my dad's brothers and their families. She complained that Marge didn't keep her house clean enough, and, according to Jane, Marge and Jerry's kids were not looked after properly. Jane did not realize that she was too fastidious to be satisfied with any standards less than her own. Consequently, she never accompanied Paul when he visited his family. A little bit of that attitude goes a long way. There was an exception, though. They did visit Aunt Cass, my father's sister, and Uncle Fuzz (Clarence). Cass was just as finicky as Jane, and Clarence was an accountant, so they passed the image test. They didn't have any children, so their house was always very clean and tidy, which met Jane's standards.

Jane, Martha, Mark, and I left for Hammond. Jane called some old friends, the Cornwells, and was planning to stay with them while we were in Hammond. When we arrived, we dropped Jane off at the Cornwells and went straight to Uncle Jerry's. Most of the family was there waiting for us to arrive. This was the first sympathy that I received other than the consolation I received from Martha the night before. My aunts and uncles knew how close I was to my dad, and they assured me that Mark, Martha, and I were the most important people in his life. I sat at the kitchen table with my aunts and uncles. Paul's brothers, Duane and Jerry, and his sister Catherine (Aunt Cass) were helping me with decisions. They helped me select pallbearers. Duane, Jerry and I made arrangements to go to the funeral home and select a casket. We also had to go to Dad's apartment in Calumet City and pick out a suit, shirt, and tie to take back to the funeral home. When we were at Dad's apartment, I took one of his suits for myself. We were the same size, and I had not packed any of my dress clothes for the weekend trip. We got what we needed and Duane, Jerry and I drove to Burnes' Funeral Home where we picked out Paul's casket and made all the other arrangements. We then headed home to call the potential pallbearers. We arranged for viewings on two evenings. Jane never did participate in any of the decision making, nor did she ever come over to Jerry's house.

I called Jane and told her that the first viewing was for the family at 3:00 p.m. the next day, followed by an open viewing from 4:00 until 8:00. When we arrived at the funeral home the next day, the director said he would take Jane and me in to see my dad. Jane seemed very controlled. She was not crying and didn't show any emotion. I remember she reached over and touched my dad on the shoulder. Meanwhile, I was kneeling on the kneeler next to his casket and I could not stop crying.

Jane finally put her arm around me and said, "It will be okay."

That was the one and only time Jane displayed any sense of sadness or any sympathy for me.

The viewings were very stressful. Dad was young and had lots of friends, so there were many people who came to express their sympathy and in one way it kept our minds off our grief. Paul's funeral was on the following morning. The funeral procession left the funeral home and headed down Hammond Avenue towards Saint Joseph Catholic Church. Jane, Martha and I rode in the family funeral car. We were followed by twenty-seven other cars. I remember I was so proud of my dad, thinking of all those folks who wanted to pay their respect to him.

Church was really tough because of our numerous family memories associated with Saint Joseph's: baptisms, first communions, confirmations, and weddings. I was really trying to keep it together, but was not doing a very good job of it. Jane was unfeeling. She showed no emotion whatsoever during the service. It was as if she was dutifully remaining stoic. She remained emotionless on the forty-five minute ride to Calvary Cemetery where Dad was laid to rest.

After the burial we somberly drove to the funeral home where we picked up Jane's car. Jane was going to drive her car back to Kankakee, and Martha and I were going to drive my dad's car back. But first, before Martha and I could go back, we had to go to Dad's apartment and pack up all his things and take them back to Kankakee. This turned out to be the hardest thing of all. With each item we packed, the realization I would never see my dad again really started to hit home. I knew that this is what he would have wanted me to do, but that didn't make the job or the drive back to Kankakee any easier.

When we arrived in Kankakee, I pulled into the driveway and parked the car. I opened the doors and started to unload all of my dad's things. Just then Jane appeared in the yard, yelling and screaming. She was frantic. She had just discovered that Paul had three life insurance policies. Two were for $1,000 each, and one was for $10,000. I was beneficiary of the two $1,000 policies, and Aunt Cass was beneficiary of the $10,000 policy. The $10,000 policy had recently had a beneficiary change. Jane had been the beneficiary, but my dad had changed it to make my Aunt Cass the beneficiary. The change had been in effect for only twenty-five minutes when my dad died. He had also left the following instructions to my Aunt Cass: The first $5,000 was to be invested for Mark's college education and the second $5,000 was to go to Martha and me at a time that Cass and Clarence thought it would be appropriate.

In the midst of Jane's hysteria, she picked up one of Dad's suitcases, threw it at me and yelled, "YOU NEVER LOVED HIM. ALL YOU EVER WANTED WAS HIS MONEY."

I was stunned. I could never figure out how a mother could do that to her son, but as I found out, that was just the beginning of things to come. I do not know what Jane was thinking; she and my Dad never discussed material things like money, to my knowledge. I never understood the root of her outburst. I guess I was the only one present at the time, and she saw me as some sort of evil person, certainly not her grieving son.

I used the two $1,000 policies to pay for my dad's funeral and clear up any small bills he had left unpaid. Martha and I returned to Collinsville, and I numbly settled in to the routine of school and work. It wasn't long before my aunt Cass notified me that Jane was suing the insurance company for the proceeds of the $10,000 insurance policy. Cass was furious, and I could not believe my mom would do such a thing. Cass had to fly back to Hammond from her home in Pittsburgh on a couple of occasions because of the lawsuit, and she made it clear to us that this was expensive, inconvenient and unnecessary. The insurance company decided that they did not want to be involved in a lawsuit, so they deposited the $10,000 with the Court. After about six months the Court awarded $5,000 to Aunt Cass and kept $5,000 for costs. Not only did Jane not get anything; she cost her son $5,000. But, as you will see, this was only the beginning of problems that she would cause.

You might wonder why my dad didn't leave any of the money to Jane. Well, first of all, I do not think he planned on dying, at least at the time; but Jane was not his center of focus at this time; it was his son and his grandson. My dad definitely wanted this money invested for future needs, and had he left it to Jane, that goal would never have been fulfilled. As it turned out, I am sure he would have been pleased to see his goals successfully completed.

Chapter Nine

Jane's First Christmas Visit

Martha, Mark, and I left Kankakee a couple of days after the funeral and returned to Collinsville. What had started out to be a fun Labor Day weekend turned out to be the worst week of my life. I was grief stricken, but managed to resume work at the bank. I would call Jane about once a week to see how she was doing. Generally, she sounded okay. She was working and trying to sort out what had just happened in her life. She told me that she was trying to figure out where she was going from this point forward. Jane didn't seem lonesome, and she never expressed any sorrow. For the most part, if she expressed any emotion, it was anger. She was angry that my dad had left her with no insurance money.

Thanksgiving was the first major holiday without my dad. Jane decided to stay in Kankakee for the holiday. I assumed that someone would invite her for dinner, but as I found out later, that didn't happen. Martha, Mark, and I were invited to Martha's brother John's in Saint Louis for the day with Martha's family.

When I learned that Jane had not received any invitations, I felt sorry for her, and I wanted to make sure that the same thing did not happen at Christmas, so we decided to celebrate Mark's first Christmas, not with Martha's family, but in Collinsville, just us and Jane. I told Jane to plan on coming for Christmas. I said it was going to be Mark's first Christmas and as his grandma, I thought that she would be excited to be a part of those memories.

About the middle of December, Jane called to tell me she was seeing someone and would like to bring him along for Christmas. At first I was really surprised. My dad had just died in September, and I was not expecting Jane to be dating or seeing anyone so soon. But then, it may really be a good thing if she had someone in Kankakee who would be a part of her life. I called her back and said that would be fine. I explained that we didn't have a lot of room in our apartment. The baby's room had a single bed that she could sleep in, but her friend would have to use the couch. Jane said that would be fine.

It wasn't very long and Christmas was upon us. Jane and her new friend Rick were driving from Kankakee and would arrive in time for Christmas eve dinner. This was going to be my first Christmas without my dad, and it was really heavy on my mind. I was somewhat uncomfortable that Jane was bringing another man with her.

The tree was up and decorated and Martha was preparing dinner when Jane and Rick arrived. When they came in, Jane introduced us to Rick, and he seemed at first glance to be a nice guy. He could not shake hands as he was holding a large box.

He handed me the box and said, "Here, this is for you for Christmas. Go ahead and open it."

Well, much to my surprise it was a case of liquor—scotch, bourbon, gin, vodka, vermouth, and rum. "Thanks," I said.

It was Mark's bedtime, so Martha took Mark upstairs. Once he was asleep we had dinner. Jane seemed happy and Rick seemed at ease. Martha was cleaning up after dinner and I wondered what I could do to make Rick feel welcome. It was getting late and I was thinking that we should start putting Mark's toys under the tree. We had bought him a hobby horse that had to be assembled.

In an effort to make Rick feel a part of the evening, I said, "Rick, have you ever put a hobby horse together?"

He thought for a minute and replied, "No, but I am sure there's enough different kinds of booze in the box that we can figure out how to mix one up."

Well, I was dumbfounded at his answer. I was referring to a child's Christmas toy and Rick thought it was some kind of a drink. That should have been some kind of a clue as to things to come. I figured I was on my own on the hobby horse assembly. I put the hobby horse together while everyone sat around and continued with the small talk. Then Rick suggested that he and Jane take a walk to help digest dinner. I couldn't wait for them to go outside.

"Well, what do you think of Rick?" I asked.

"If Paul were here he would have been right down there with you putting that hobby horse together and helping us plan Mark's first Christmas," Martha responded. "I think he's really into drinking, too," she added.

I was really missing my dad. When Jane and Rick returned from their walk, it was time for bed. Martha fixed up the couch for Rick, and she and Jane and I went up stairs to bed.

Christmas morning I woke up early because I was excited about Mark's first Christmas. When I got out of bed, I heard some strange sounds coming from downstairs in the living room. I assured myself that the noises I was hearing could not be what it sounded like, but I was becoming more suspicious with each step. As I reached the stairs where I could see down into the living room, the sounds became very pronounced and more definable. I took a double take and got the shock of my life. Jane was on the couch with Rick. They were both nude and looked like a pair of Sumo Wrestlers doing their thing. I could not believe my eyes. How could they be doing this on Christmas morning when Martha would be bringing Mark would downstairs at any moment! What about the memory of my dad? I tried to compose myself. Then I told them both to pack up their stuff and get out. They got dressed, packed up what little amount they had, and headed for the door. Some Christmas morning!

Nothing else was ever said until I was talking to Jane some time later, and I asked about Rick. She told me that after they got back to Kankakee, he told her that he was married and that he had four kids. I thought even less of him when I learned that he chose not to be with his family at Christmas.

Chapter Ten

Jane moves to Troy

It was the first part of May, and we had not seen Jane since Christmas. I was now working at National Tea Company when Martha received a call from Saint Mary's Hospital in Kankakee. They were looking for me. Jane had been admitted. They would not say what the problem was, just that they needed to talk to Dennis. Martha contacted me at work, relayed the message, and told me to call right away. The hospital informed me that Jane had taken an overdose of sleeping pills in an attempt to commit suicide, evidently changed her mind, and called emergency services. They informed me that she was under suicide watch, and I needed to come to the hospital since I was the next of kin. I nervously explained it would take me nearly five hours to drive to Kankakee, but they repeated that I should come. I explained the situation to my boss and left immediately. When I arrived at the hospital, I was given Jane's room number. Upon arriving on her floor, I noticed a uniformed officer outside one of the rooms. As I got closer, I realized that the officer was outside of Jane's room. I identified myself and asked why he was stationed there. The officer told me that he was assigned suicide watch and that Jane was considered a suicide risk.

When I entered the room I was surprised at what I saw. Jane was on all fours in a hospital bed with high railings on both sides almost like a baby in a crib. Jane had a tendency to act like a child on some occasions, and sometimes she would even talk like a child.

Shaken, I walked over to the bed and asked, "Are you okay?"

"I'm just fine," she snapped in a childlike tone.

"Well, you do not sound fine to me, and you sure as hell do not look like you're fine." I retorted. "What are you doing in here like this? What were you thinking?" I was getting irritated. "Mom," I explained, "I just had to take off work and drive five hours for this. If you're just fine, then why don't you start acting fine?"

"It was all a big misunderstanding," she said, "but they won't discharge me until I sign a paper stating that I will see a psychiatrist."

"What do you plan to do?"

"I am going to sign their damn paper and get the hell out of here as soon as I can."

"Then do you plan to follow through with the psychiatrist?"

"Hell no, but they don't know that. I just want to go home."

"You obviously need some help. You can't keep drinking and smoking three packs of Camels a day and eating goofy pills and expect to have a productive life. Why don't you move down around Collinsville close to us?" I suggested. *What the hell was I thinking?* "I am sure you can get a job there and be near your family and grandson."

I told her that Martha was expecting another child, so she could be near her two grandchildren. I also told her we had purchased a lot and planned to build a new house. She indicated that she didn't have the money to pay for the move, so I offered to pay for a moving van and help her find a place to live. I continued to encourage her, telling her that Martha and I would pay her rent and her security deposit until she got a job. Unfortunately, she took me up on my offer. Now that I look back, I really believe that was her plan all along.

Martha found a nice little one bedroom apartment in Troy, Illinois, a little town about five miles from our house in Collinsville. Once Jane got moved and settled, I tried to encourage her to start looking for a job. On June 6, 1964, Martha delivered our second son Michael. Mark was now two and Martha was busy with a new baby and a two-year-old. Jane would arrive at our house everyday around 10:00 a.m. and stay all day, but all she would do is sit at the kitchen table and chain smoke. She generally went home around 10:00 p.m. in the evening. She never made any attempt to look for a job or help Martha with the kids. In fact, to make things worse, while she was sitting around smoking, she was telling Martha all the things she was doing wrong as far as taking caring for the children and keeping the house. Jane never felt that the kids were clean enough and she complained that the house was messy; however, she never lifted a hand to help. This continued for about three months.

I urged her to look for work and told her that Martha and I could not continue to support her because we had a young family we were raising. Martha and I were in our mid-twenties, and Jane was in her mid-forties and very able bodied. She had held a job in Kankakee and was capable of finding another job and getting back on her feet. I felt that being near her family was giving her the support she needed to take care of herself, but that didn't seem to be the case. My encouragement was to no avail. She continued camping out at our house and alienating herself from Martha while making friends with some of our neighbors. Making friends wasn't so bad, but the neighbors began telling us that we didn't meet with Jane's approval. She was badmouthing us to them.

"What's the matter with your mother," they would ask. "You have been so hospitable towards her and she complains about the two of you all the time." They couldn't believe her behavior and neither could Martha and I.

Things had reached a point that I felt Jane needed some of my tough love (shock therapy). So one beautiful summer Sunday when Jane was coming over for dinner, I suggested that she come a little early because "I have some place I would like to take you."

When Jane arrived, I suggested, "Come on, get in the car. We're going for a ride."

Alton, Illinois, is about twenty-five miles away and is home to one of Illinois' state mental hospitals. When we arrived at the hospital, the gates were open and we were free to drive around on the hospital grounds. As might be expected on a nice Sunday afternoon, many of the patients were outside on the benches enjoying the beautiful day.

Jane kept looking around and finally inquired, "What are we doing here?"

I stopped the car, opened the glove compartment, and removed a large white envelope. "Mom," I said, "I have all the papers necessary to have you committed to this place for the rest of your life. They've been signed by two doctors, and if I sign them, I can commit you to this institution right now for what may be the remainder of your life."

Thank God, she never asked to see the letter because it was a big bluff. However, she felt that I had had enough. Jane also knew that I had talked to Dr. Lang and Dr. Urlich, the two doctors with whom she had worked for several years. Jane also knew that the doctors knew that she had taken all the pills, so I am sure she felt that is who had signed the (fake) admitting forms. She became very serious.

"Martha and I cannot keep supporting you like this. You've got two weeks to get a job, quit drinking and take control of your life or you're going to find yourself here."

Jane just looked at me and didn't say a word. I think she knew my demands were serious and she was smart enough to figure it was time to change her life. Within two weeks, she was employed at the Edwardsville Country Club as a bookkeeper and office manager.

Jane did continue to stop over almost every day after work for dinner. I thought that she would be a big help to Martha with the kids, but instead she was like a third older kid who drank and smoked. Things weren't exactly working out as planned. I had stopped working for National Tea and was traveling selling Yellow Pages in central and southern Illinois and was only home on the weekends. There was an exception when we were working in the Collinsville area, about four months out of the year.

Jane became friends with the lady across the street from us. She began coming over after work and would then go over to Glenna's house and complain about Martha.

She would confide to Glenna, "I don't know why Dennie married that girl. She sure is not a very good mother in my opinion."

Later Glenna would tell Martha what Jane had said. When I got home I heard it all over again. However, Martha never confronted Jane to the best of my knowledge.

Something else came to our attention not long after Jane moved to Troy. There had been clues to this while Jane was in Kankakee, but I dismissed them until Jane overdosed on the sleeping pills. I had received anonymous calls on several occasions from someone in Kankakee, while Jane was still living there. The caller said that Jane was abusing prescription drugs. We thought it was some trouble-making neighbor who didn't like Jane. The attempted suicide, though, made me realize that Jane did indeed have a problem with prescription drugs, and that is one of the reasons that I thought the move to our area was advisable for her. After Jane moved to Troy, we noticed that she made frequent trips to the pharmacy. She had allergies and needed pills and salves and also would take terpin hydrate and codeine for her cough (which was probably from the Camels). We didn't think too much of it. Martha and I were completely unfamiliar with anyone who had ever abused prescription drugs, so the clues that Jane displayed to us were left unheeded at the time.

As I said before, Jane visited nearly every evening. We were settling into sort of a routine. It wasn't all misery. When I was in town working and at home at night, we had our pleasant times. We would cook out. Jane and Martha would frequently tackle some small project, and of course, we all enjoyed watching Mark and Michael play and grow. But through all of this, one never knew when Jane would throw one of her barbs in our direction. Just when we would begin to relax and think things were going well, Jane would become very critical of us. We wouldn't keep enough milk on hand; we wouldn't keep scrubbing the kids hands when they got dirty, (she, however, would rub them raw and clean their ears about every ten minutes or so). We didn't keep the kids on a rigid schedule. We stretched our budget too thin. (That was a rich one . . . we could have managed a bit better if we had not been helping her with her finances.)

During these rather peaceful and uneventful months, Jane would ask to borrow our car. Our new Chrysler was much nicer than her old Buick Special, and she wanted to drive over to Scott Air Force Base. Her request usually occurred on Saturday nights. She told us that she had befriended someone at the Officers Club at the base and wanted to meet him for drinks. I thought of the past and how she and my dad used to frequent Sully's in Kankakee. She always enjoyed nightlife, so Martha and I agreed that Jane would take the Chrysler to Belleville and have an enjoyable night. These trips to Belleville became part of the routine. We were glad that she was developing some kind of social life. We were relieved not to have her depend on us for everything.

It was a beautiful summer Saturday evening. Martha and I had put the kids to bed and were relaxing on the patio. Jane had gone to Scott Air Force Base. The phone rang and I answered it.

"Is this Dennis Solon," the voice on the line inquired.

"Yes, it is."

"Are you the son of Jane Solon?"

"Yes, I am"

"Well, I am the commander of Scott Air Force Base here in Belleville. I'm calling to tell you that I would like you to keep your mother off of the base."

I was shocked. "Is there a problem with her being there?"

"Yes, there is" Your mother has been visiting the Officers' Club and is prostituting herself for drinks and cigarettes."

"I'll take care of it." I answered, and hung up the phone.

I did not want to believe what I had just heard, but I knew it was true. I relayed the message to Martha, and she was as shocked and outraged as I. Of course, I would see to it that Jane wouldn't go back to the base.

I didn't know what to do about my mom's behavior. I thought about calling my Aunt Mary K. in Chicago, but she would never believe me, and I didn't want her to know what her sister had been doing. I never did confront my mom about going back to Scott. We just told her that it would be better if she didn't use our car anymore. I'm sure she thought we were just being selfish.

This situation plagued me. I didn't know what to do. I decided to confide in Martha's dad. We were going to Gillespie the next weekend, and I was eager to see what kind of advice he could give me. He was familiar with our situation with Jane. Martha had complained to him about her behavior, but he always reminded her to "be respectful of Dennis's mother." He had never offered an opinion of any kind regarding our moving Jane to Troy, and I do not think he was aware of the extent of the financial help we were giving her. I told him of Jane's trips to Scott and the phone call I received.

"What should I do?" I said.

"Dennis, there is nothing you can do. This is not your fault. Just keep her off the base and hope that she straightens up."

That's pretty much how I handled it.

I began to think I was nuts to have ever tried to help my mom. On many occasions, I would look up toward heaven and ask my Dad why the hell he did this to Martha and me.

The trips to Belleville did stop, but Jane's visits to us continued. Things settled into a routine again. Jane was still coming over most nights and weekends, and she pretty much depended on us for her social life.

When she came in the boys would always say, "Hi Grandma."

She always replied, "I am not old enough to be a grandma, so JUST CALL ME JANE!"

She also continued her friendship with Glenna across the street. Her frequent visits over there were beginning to extend into the dinner hour. Jane began staying at Glenna's for dinner and then long into the evening hours (she must have been tiring of us). This was beginning to annoy Glenna's husband, Tony, and he complained to us. Now we were going to have trouble with our neighbors. What next?

I noticed that Jane was selling some of her crystal and silver to Glenna so that she could make a little extra cash for herself. She never seemed to have enough money, yet she continued purchasing expensive clothes, probably more expensive than she could afford, saying that she needed a nice wardrobe for work. It was getting more and more difficult for her to maintain the lifestyle she wanted. I could not afford to give her any more money. She was frustrated, and so was I. There did not seem to be any way to avoid taking care of my mother. With some luck, perhaps things would settle down and we could maintain peace with our neighbors. Maybe Jane would just become my mom again and a fit grandma for our little boys. This was not to be the case.

The next "incident" took place in the fall. I was working on the Yellow Page Directory for Centralia, Illinois. It was a beautiful fall day, work had gone well, and I checked into the motel with the rest of the yellow page crew. There was a message there from Martha. No emergency, but I was to call her as soon as I could. I thought I would give her a call and top off a good day. That was not to be. I dialed home and Martha answered.

"I am so glad you called, because I have had one hell of a day! You're mom's really done it this time."

"What's up?" I answered.

Well, it's a long story, but you're going to hear the entire thing! I got a frantic phone call about 9:30 this morning from your mom. She was on her way to work and was pulled over by a traffic cop for speeding. As usual, she smarted off to the officer, pissed him off, as she is so adept at doing, and he hauled her off to a judge in Belleville!

"Oh shit!" I said.

"Oh wait, I'm just getting started! She told the judge that the officer tried to rape her. The judge threw her in jail! Of course, she got to make one phone call and she picked ME!"

"Oh shit!"

"Well, she told me that bail was set at $80, and I needed to come down to Belleville and bail her out." "Where in the hell was I going to get $80 cash?" "Dennie, I had to go ask Jim Kelly for $80 to get your mom out of jail"

"Oh my God, what did he say?"

"He was so sweet. He gave me the money and told me that we could pay him back whenever we could." "Can you imagine what I must have looked like going into his office with a four-year-old, a two-year-old, and me as big as a barn, pregnant, asking for $80 to bail my mother-in-law out of jail?"

"No, I can't."

"You think it's over, don't you?"

"I hope so." I was numb.

"Well, I got the money, put the kids in the car, drove to Belleville and bailed her out. She didn't even say 'thank you.' We got in the car and she told me to go to Collinsville to pick up her car. When we got to Collinsville to the police station where her car was supposedly parked, she began bitching, "My car's not here; they stole my car." By the way, she also bitched all the way from Belleville to Collinsville. I told her that I would go in to the police station and see if they could tell me where her car was. When I went in there and told them who I was, I could just see it in their eyes . . . I was with a kook!" They told me that her car was in Caseyville, not Collinsville . . . that "the lady" was confused, and if I drove over to Caseyville, I would find her car in front of the Caseyville police station and that the attendant inside would have her keys. Well, I went out and told Jane. She kept on bitching. She was driving me crazy. When we got to the police station, I got her keys for her, and she drove her car and I drove my car back to our house. She still never thanked me."

"Oh, my God!" I said. "You really had one shitty day."

"Oh, it's not over yet!" Martha said.

"What do you mean?"

"When we got back to the house, your mom parked her car in front, like she always does. She came on inside. I think it was about 1:00. I fixed us some lunch and put Mike to bed. We were just sitting around and your mom was still carrying on about what happened, and how dumb the cops were when Glenna called. She said, "Martha, Dennie's mom's car is on fire!" Sure enough, we looked out and black smoke was pouring out of the back windows of the car. The entire back of your mom's car burned up!"

"Jesus! It's ruined? What caused it?"

"She threw a cigarette butt out of the window, and it landed in the backseat. She didn't pick up on it, and it set the car on fire. The car's ruined."

"Oh shit, what did you do?"

"I had to have the damn thing towed away! Dennie, this shit is getting old! I don't know how much more I can take."

"Yeah, I know. Hang in there. I'll be home this weekend. I'll take care of Jim Kelly. I'll figure something out about my mom." Then I reminded her that I love her.

Well, I thanked Jim Kelly for helping Martha, but I didn't have any answers when it came to my mom. She had to borrow one of our cars to get to work, and she also informed us that she would not be paying for a car that was burned up.

"Mom," I said, "Martha and I cosigned on that car. The loan has to be paid."

"Well, I'm not paying!" she replied. Once again, we were stuck with another bill for Mom.

Jane continued working and coming over to the house. I wanted to distance myself from her and give Martha a break. Maybe going out on weekends might help. Martha and I began going out on Saturday nights. One of the girls in the neighborhood would come over and babysit with the boys. We would usually go over to St. Louis, have dinner and take in a movie. On one particular Saturday evening when we arrived home, Jane's car was in the driveway. We immediately wondered why Jane would be over at our house when we had a babysitter. When we went in, we found that the babysitter was gone and Jane was in the bedroom with Mark and Mike. She was drunk, and she had gotten the boys up. She had them on her lap, rocking them and telling them that their Mommy and Daddy don't love them as much as Grandma does. Martha and I were furious.

"Where's the baby sitter?" We asked.

"I sent her home." Jane replied, slurring her words and obviously drunk. "She doesn't take good care of them. I've been over here before and had to take over for her, didn't she tell you? You need to hire baby sitters that are more capable."

"Go in to the kitchen, Mom," I demanded, so that Martha could put the boys back to bed. It didn't take long for Martha to get the kids settled. She went in to the family room while I handled Jane.

I told my mom to wait in the kitchen and that I wanted to talk to her. I was at the end of my patience. I was desperate and furious. I felt that I was backed into a corner. There was no escaping my mom. I went to the garage and got my Colt 45 automatic pistol. It was loaded. I went in to the kitchen and told Jane that I couldn't take her drinking and her constant meddling in our lives.

"You have been complaining and totally miserable ever since we moved you down here," I said. I handed her the loaded Colt 45 automatic pistol. "PLEASE PLEASE, do me a favor. Go out to the front yard and blow your damn head off. I beg you . . . please."

She just set the gun down and walked out.

The next day, I received a phone call from our babysitter's mother. "Dennis, please do not call my daughter to baby sit for your children any more."

"Why?" I asked.

She explained, "Every time you and Martha go out and Sherry is babysitting, your mother comes over and gets in your liquor, gets drunk, and tells Sherry what horrible parents you and Martha are."

I told her I was sorry and I would see to it that it didn't ever happen again, but she insisted that Sherry would not be babysitting for us any more. Embarrassed, I said that I understood. But now we were left with the dilemma of finding a new sitter for the kids and having another neighbor alienated.

Chapter Eleven

Moving West

Nothing ever lasts forever, and that was true for our family. Martha was pregnant with our third child and things were changing with my job. In December, 1966, Martha gave birth to our third son John, and after looking at what was available and considering all of the options in the job market, I decided to take a Job with Herff Jones Co. as a manufacturer's representative. This was a great opportunity, but it required moving to Colorado Springs, Colorado. This was also a chance to get away from all of the problems with Jane and just be our own family. In the early part of summer of 1966, we sold our house and loaded everything we had in a huge U-haul truck, packed up the boys, and headed for Colorado Springs. Jane had never seen any mountains, and Colorado Springs was so pretty I looked forward to having her come and visit. However, neither one of us ever had the extra money for a plane ticket, and she couldn't get the time off from work at the country club, so she never did get a chance to visit.

The only real contact with Jane while we were in Colorado was by phone. We called each other about every ten days or so. From the phone calls, Jane seemed to be doing fine.

She continued to visit Glenna frequently and made a new friend named Russ who lived across the street from her in Troy. It was a joy to live without the frequent frustrations that Jane caused. We were experiencing a welcome sense of freedom. Jane was not there to harass us, or so I thought.

My job required me to do some traveling, and on a trip back to Herff Jones in Indianapolis, I had a short layover at O'Hare airport in Chicago. O'Hare is one of the busiest airports in the U.S. While walking from one terminal to another, I heard my name being paged. I was in shock. All I could think was that something was wrong with Martha or the boys. I went to a courtesy phone and identified myself. The operator asked me to hold for an emergency call. Now I was more worried than ever. When I got the connection, much to my surprise, it was Jane. I asked why she would have me paged at O'Hare and what was so important that it could not wait till I got to Indianapolis.

Jane was quick with her answer. "Well, I just came from the doctor's office and he told me I was terminal and I thought you should know right away."

When I pressed her for more information about why she was "terminal" and who the doctor was that gave her this diagnosis, she gave me very vague answers about having some sort of cancer. It became obvious that she was fabricating the entire situation, and as I listened to her slurring her words, I realized that she had been drinking.

"What do you think?" she asked.

I could not believe the worry she put me through with that page and phone call. I was so irritated that I snapped back, saying, "We're all terminal!" I then hung up the phone and headed for the gate to catch the plane.

Chapter Twelve

Ohio Christmas Stories

After only one year in Colorado, Herff-Jones transferred me to Dayton, Ohio. We were only six hours from Troy. This would make it easier and less expensive for Jane to come and visit. Since our phone conversations (excluding the one at O'Hare) always seemed pretty positive, I surmised that Jane was doing okay; therefore, we were looking forward to spending some time with her. The first Christmas we were going to be in Dayton was 1967. We had planned to buy her an airline ticket from St. Louis to Dayton, but we received a call from Martha's brother John who lived in St. Louis. He told us that he and Colette had to drive to Washington D.C. over Christmas, and they would be traveling right through Dayton. They wondered if we would keep their two daughters, Francine and Michele, over Christmas. The girls could have a nice visit with our family, while John and Colette took care of business in Washington. Of course, we readily agreed to watch the girls. It would give us all a chance to spend the holiday together. Then it dawned on us that they were traveling right through Troy. We asked if they had room to bring Jane and that it would save us the cost of an airline ticket. "No problem," they said. They would arrive a couple of days before Christmas.

As the time got closer, we all got more excited about seeing everyone since we had been away for over a year. Martha had decorated the house for Christmas; the tree was beautiful; the presents were wrapped and under the tree. We were eager to celebrate the holiday with family. It was about 11:00 p.m. a couple of days before Christmas when John's car pulled in the driveway. I called Martha and the boys and told them that Uncle John, Aunt Colette, the girls, and Jane were here. We all headed for the door, expecting to see happy faces and trade lots of hugs and kisses. Much to our surprise, the greeting was the exact opposite. The girls came in and went straight through the entry to the family room, never saying a word.

Next, was Colette who looked at Martha and declared, "That woman is impossible!" She was followed by John.

He looked at Martha and blurted, "Do not ever ask me to take that woman anywhere ever again!"

Martha and I were surprised and a bit shaken up. Jane, who never did move too fast, was still getting out of the car, so I went out to greet her and give her a hug.

She looked at me and said, "Those people are impossible! Don't ever make me ride with them anywhere ever again!"

"What was wrong with everyone?" I wondered as Jane and I approached the house.

Once in the house, we sorted luggage and assigned bedrooms. Jane was in the back bedroom getting settled and in the kitchen John explained what had taken place.

When they left Troy, he said, Jane was in the back seat with the girls. She immediately lit up a cigarette. At first John asked her not to smoke in the car as they were not smokers and it was a confined area.

Jane responded with a stern "no" and indicated that she enjoyed smoking.

In an effort to be somewhat agreeable, John asked her if she would please crack her window so some of the smoke could escape out the window.

Again, Jane responded, "Of course not. Don't you realize how cold it is out there?"

I knew how unpleasant Jane could be, so I quickly realized how tense the atmosphere must have been during that six-hour drive. John and Colette, a normally very patient and tolerant pair, had persevered through Jane's endless biting remarks. Jane had "burned her bridges" with another set of people.

Instead of engaging in the late-night festivities that usually are associated with reunions, we all decided that we were tired and went to bed. Hopefully, the next day would bring a more pleasant atmosphere.

The next morning John and Colette had a quick breakfast and then left for Washington. They didn't say any more about the drive from Troy. That morning Michele and Francine entertained Mark, Mike, and John.

They were a great help to Martha, and just having the kids around the house while preparing for Christmas put us in a better mood than we had been in the night before when the atmosphere was so strained. We knew we were up for a wonderful Christmas. The girls were a little tense when Jane surfaced, which was about noon. We thought it a little odd that she slept so late, but figured she was just tired from working and last night's journey. Thankfully, she didn't bring up the trip either.

We did discover that Jane's habits while on vacation varied from when she was working. She would stay up until 2:00-3:00 a.m. and then sleep until 2:00-3:00 p.m. in the afternoon. Once she arose, she would chain smoke. She was smoking heavier than ever. Martha and I were both smokers, so of course we were tolerant of anyone smoking in the house. That was the way things were in 1967. However, Jane had developed a habit of leaving her burning cigarettes in the many available ashtrays in our house. The cigarettes would burn down and it was not uncommon to have a burned-down nub fall out of an ashtray and on to the wood coffee table. Burn marks began to spring up on our Ethan Allan wood tables. We also watched in astonished horror while cigarettes would burn down in her fingers, sometimes falling on the couch or chair, as the case may be, and nearly smolder in the furniture. We had to watch her every second. As the evenings wore on, I would get so tired that I would finally give up and go to bed because the kids would be up first thing in the morning. However, Martha was always afraid that Jane was going to burn the house down around us, so she would stay up with Jane until the wee hours of the morning, listening to her vicious complaints about her so-called friends and acquaintances in Troy and the idiots who she worked with. During these diatribes, she would imbibe in too many bourbons and water and smoke too many cigarettes. Martha would finally convince Jane to go to bed, then come to bed exhausted, knowing that she would have to be up in a few hours with the kids. Jane even repeated this scenario on Christmas Eve, retiring drunk about 3:00a.m and rising around 3:00p.m. on Christmas day. We had to hold up Christmas dinner until "her highness" was ready. When she arrived at the table with her bourbon and water, she announced that she really did not want to eat too much. She had one slice of turkey and two pieces of celery. During dinner, she stated that she was concerned because she thought that she might have cancer because she was losing weight.

Martha suggested, "Maybe if you eat a little more, you might not lose weight."

Jane's response was biting and quick. "I refuse to overeat," she said.

Needless to say, we were relieved when Jane caught the plane back to St. Louis. Her departure was well received by all.

Once again I looked up and said, "Dad, you really stuck it to me by dying way too soon. What did I do to deserve this?"

The rest of the holiday with just us and the kids was restful and peaceful.

We didn't see Jane very often for the next several years. Summers we would make trips to Illinois to visit Martha's dad in Gillespie. There we would see her sister Mary and her husband Jerome and visit John and Colette in St. Louis. Of course, we would go to Troy and visit Jane.

I mentioned before that Jane had a friend named Russ who lived across the street from her in Troy. I noticed that their friendship had blossomed. Jane would tell us about how nice Russ was to her and that sometimes he lent her money. He would pay for her to have her car washed and would sometimes meet her for coffee on Saturdays. Russ's wife would never join them for coffee. Jane explained that Russ's wife didn't do too much, just stayed around the house. Jane didn't wish to have any sort of relationship with her, but she liked Russ. I smelled trouble, but said nothing.

Each year, we would invite Jane for the holidays. Each year, I hoped for a pleasant, non-eventful holiday with Jane, but that was never the case. I would attempt to advise Jane and tell her the danger of drinking and smoking and falling asleep, and the possibility of burning down the house. The advice really didn't seem to matter. Her behavior was not going to change. If I complained, she would get the phone book and start calling the airlines to get a return flight home because we were being mean to her.

Once Martha woke me about 4:00 a.m. and said, "Your mom's out cold on the bathroom floor, naked as a jaybird. I covered her with a towel, but you need to go in there and get her up."

I went into the bathroom and there was my mother on the floor between the tub and the commode. We didn't want the kids to wake up and see her in that condition. We struggled, pushed, pulled, and finally got her back in bed. This must have looked like a scene from a Laurel and Hardy movie. Jane must have passed out when she was on the commode. We said nothing of it the following morning. Just another Christmas with Grandma.

In spite of all the problems, I always felt guilty about leaving Jane alone at Christmas, so each year I would send another airplane ticket, and each year she would show up.

I will never forget the year that our neighborhood friends were having a Christmas party, and they invited Martha and me. I explained that we best decline, as my mom was coming for Christmas, and it would probably be best if we stayed close to home. Well, our friends insisted that we come and bring Jane with us. We finally agreed and went to the party. I figured that if there was a problem we were only three houses away, and we could walk home in five minutes. Les and Nettie, our hosts, were serving drinks and the usual Christmas party fare. Nettie had the house and tree decorated beautifully and everyone was in a festive mood. Our neighbors were being especially nice to Jane.

I never realized how much Jane was drinking until Les the host remarked, "Man, your mom must have two hollow legs to be able to hold that much bourbon."

It was at about that same time I heard a huge crash with a lot of breaking glass. I turned to see Jane lying on the floor. She lay in the midst of broken ornaments and strands of lights. Nettie's beautiful tree—demolished—lay on the floor beside her. There Jane was, on her back in all the glass and mess; her legs pointing straight to heaven and her dress up around her hips. All the men were rushing to pick her up and brush off the glass ornaments and pieces of the lights. I was so embarrassed, I could have died.

Once on her feet, Jane looked down at the huge mess and proclaimed to the guests, "Well, it was an ugly tree anyway!"

At that point I went well past embarrassed to mortified and totally pissed. Martha and I apologized and ushered Jane home.

The next day, I tried the same old lecture. "Mom, you need to stop the drinking and cut back on the cigarettes, too. It's causing real problems for everyone, and it's not helping your health either. Think about what happened last night."

"It's my life and I'll live it the way I want to. You're not going to tell me what to do. Les and Nettie invited too many people for their little house. If they would have planned better, their tree wouldn't have been knocked over."

My advice fell on deaf ears.

A few days after Christmas, Martha and I took Jane to the airport and sent her back home. We were once again relieved to see her go and thankful that she had to get back to work. The whole time Jane was with us, she never spent any real time with the boys. I would have thought that since it was Christmas, she would have wanted to be involved with the kids, but that was not to be the case.

Martha and I always went out of our way at Christmas to build family traditions and make the kids understand the meaning of Christmas and all the joy that went with the season. As we look back, we did accomplish our family traditions, but one of the things that really stuck with the kids was all the chaos, frustration and anger that Jane brought every time she came to visit.

Mark, Martha, Mike, Dennis, Shannon & John
on vacation at the Sears Tower

One of Jane's visits

Jane with Shannon, John, Mike and Mark

Chapter Thirteen

Jane Moves to Dayton

Jane continued to drink heavily and never did give up the Camels. Her health had continuously gone downhill. Her doctors in Illinois told her that she would really benefit from much-needed cardiac bypass surgery. The surgery was very serious and we knew that there would be an extended recovery period. Jane did not have anyone that she could depend on to help her after the surgery. As an only child, I felt responsible for helping Jane. Martha agreed, and in 1978 we decided to move Jane to Dayton so that she could undergo her surgery and recovery while living close to us.

The plans were set in place to help Jane move. Martha and I drove to Troy early in the morning the day the movers were to arrive. This day started out like many others where Jane was involved. Martha and I had a very positive feeling about moving Jane to Dayton. We had found a nice apartment in our neighborhood only about six blocks from our house in Centerville, a Dayton suburb. Because of the close proximity to our house, we felt that Jane would be able to be involved with meals, the kids, and family activities while still maintaining her independence in her own place. As usual, when things involve Jane, they never seem to work out as planned; Jane always has a way of putting a damper on everything.

As I mentioned, we arrived at Jane's place in Troy just before the movers were scheduled to arrive. Jane was supposed to have packed her belongings such as dishes, household items, and personal things. The movers would then load the boxes and furniture. Much to our surprise, Jane hadn't packed one item, even though she had been given three weeks' notice and was much in favor of the move. When we walked in her place, she was sitting in a chair, smoking a cigarette and watching TV. She had not done one thing to prepare for the move. At that point, my mood changed very quickly from one of positive feelings to total disgust. It just seemed that Jane had a way to turning any good situation into a total disaster.

Martha and I were forced to get boxes and feverishly started packing all of Jane's belongings. When the movers arrived, we had barely made a dent in the packing. The entire time Jane was almost out of touch with what was happening. She was no help. I felt she would be excited about moving to Dayton and being involved with us and her grandchildren, but that wasn't the case. The movers were very helpful, but Martha and I were nearly frantic trying to keep up with them. They finally started loading Jane's furniture. When they lifted Jane's mattress and springs from her bed frame, I was shocked with what I saw. Empty whiskey and gin bottles were carelessly thrown under the bed. Jane's drinking problem was more serious than I thought. This, coupled with her use of prescription medication, was a recipe for disaster.

Once everything was out of the apartment, Martha started to clean, dad and I loaded Jane's clothes and small items into our cars for the trip back to Dayton. By 6:00 p.m., the truck was fully loaded. The chaos and confusion was over. The drivers were leaving for Dayton the following day, but we decided to drive back to Dayton that evening. We could be home by 11:00, and the kids were excited about seeing Jane.

When we arrived, the kids all came to greet us. They first approached Jane, expecting hugs and kisses. Well, that was not to be. Jane ignored them, asking me for a drink so that she could unwind from the trip. I felt bad for the kids and couldn't help but think if my Dad would have been there instead of Jane he would have given them a lot of attention.

It was late, so we told the kids to get ready for bed. We always had a tradition that everyone got a kiss good night, so it was very natural for the kids to go to Grandma to give her a kiss.

As the kids approached her and said "Good night, Grandma," she gave each one a peck on the cheek and said "Call me Jane, I'm not ready to be a grandma."

I was disappointed for them once again.

The next morning, Martha and I took Jane over to the apartment we had rented. It was a four-unit two story building with two units up and two units down. The building was in a very nice residential neighborhood in Centerville. Jane's unit was on the second floor on the right. The apartment was a one-bedroom, one-bath unit with a dining area and a twelve by sixteen living room. There were plenty of windows, so the place was bright and had pleasant neighborhood views with lots of trees. The kitchen was attractive and equipped with fairly new appliances. We were happy that we had found the place and we could tell that Jane was actually pleased. We found a chair for Jane to sit on while Martha and I unpacked her clothes and personal items, putting them where she wanted. The day passed pretty pleasantly. That afternoon, the kids rode their bikes up to the apartment to see how everything was going. It was an exciting time for them. They were eager to help.

Jane's reaction was "Please don't touch that."

It didn't take long for the kids to lose interest in the move. They hopped on their bikes and rode the six blocks through the neighborhood back home to play with their friends.

The moving van arrived early in the afternoon. The furniture was unloaded by 4:30 and everything was in place. That evening, Jane came for dinner and the next day, Martha planned to show her around the area so that she would be familiar with the locations of grocery stores, pharmacies, and medical buildings.

That week, I helped Jane find a local doctor who would, in turn, recommend her to a cardiologist. I also helped her set up a local bank account. She became acclimated very quickly. She spent most of her evenings at our house and shared dinner with us. I noticed that she was moving more slowly than usual. She was only 64 years of age, but moved much more slowly than most 64-year-olds.

"Maybe it is just me," I thought. We are so much younger and always in a rush. "Maybe it's just us."

But as I observed my mom, she seemed incredibly slow in everything she did. Through the years, Jane had always taken her time, moving much slower than us, much to our frustration. She had always been the last one ready when we were going anywhere. She could take 45 minutes to make a sandwich. She had always been the last one to sit down at the dinner table for family dinners. She had always been the last one to finish eating. But now she was even worse. When dinner was served and everyone was finished eating, the kids would be asking to be excused and Jane would just be getting started. She would push her food around on her plate and almost never took a bite. At first, we would wait for her to finish, but after a few weeks when she didn't speed up, we would have to excuse ourselves while leaving her at the table alone to finish. Jane thought this was terribly rude of us, but to be honest, it couldn't be helped. If we stayed until Jane finished dinner, it might be another 30 minutes. Kids have studies and bedtimes. I felt that they were very tolerant of their grandma's eccentricities, so we allowed them to go on with their evening's activities and responsibilities without succumbing to Jane's wishes. Martha would clean up the kitchen and chat with Jane, but sometimes the kitchen work would be completely finished while Jane was still eating. If that was the case, Martha would go on in the family room and leave Jane to finish her dinner alone. When this occurred, I remember seeing Jane taking her dishes to the sink and washing them. She would stand there with her hands in that steaming water, and she would seem to be in a trance.

I would touch her on the shoulder and say, "Mom, Mom!"

She would awaken, startled, and pull her hands out of the water. Miraculously she was never burned.

At the time neither Martha nor I had any idea about the drugs that Jane was taking every day. That fact that Jane may have been abusing prescription drugs and over the counter drugs did not occur to us. We just attributed these actions to her old eccentricities. Jane was now under the care of a cardiologist and would get prescriptions to control her blood pressure, heart, pulmonary problems, and chest pains. We didn't monitor the drugs she was taking, so to this day I am still not sure of what her prescriptions were. However, Martha and I began to suspect that she was abusing drugs because she would mention the various pharmacies she visited. It seemed she was familiar with every pharmacy in Centerville. I recalled the abuse of drugs in the past. She had abused prescription drugs while in Kankakee, taken an overdose of sleeping pills, and apparently abused alcohol ever since my dad died. She was a mess. But now this "mess" had resulted in some serious health problems. At sixty-four, Jane had noticeable pulmonary issues in addition to a weak heart. Just walking to her car would result in shortness of breath and chest pains even though she was taking medication. Yet, she continued to smoke and drink.

At this point Jane was collecting Social Security, and we were picking up the remainder of her financial obligations. She was not able to work because her health was too poor.

She came over most afternoons to visit with Martha when the kids arrived home from school. She didn't have much to do with the boys, but she enjoyed Shannon, who was in second grade at the time. Sometimes she would take Shannon for ice cream or a light supper at Denny's Restaurant or Friendly's Ice Cream Shop. Shannon always enjoyed this time with her grandma, and I am sure Jane enjoyed these moments with Shannon as well.

Shannon was about eight years old and after one such outing when Jane dropped Shannon off at home, I asked Shannon if she had a good time with Grandma.

"Yes," she responded, but then she looked up in the air and moved her head from left to right very quickly. She did this repeatedly.

"What are you doing?" I inquired.

"When I ride with Grandma, this is what I do."

"What are you talking about?

"Grandma likes to run all the red lights, and I just keep watching them as we go flying past."

Was Shannon correct in her assessment of Grandma's driving habits? One day the opportunity of discovery presented itself. I was pulling out of my office parking lot when I saw Jane driving past in her pink Buick. I decided to follow her. She ran four red lights in a row. She must have been oblivious to every one of them. I had imported a driving menace to Centerville. Needless to say, Shannon did not take any more road trips with Grandma.

Then there were Jane's unannounced trips to my real estate office. I was co-owner of Cobblestone Real Estate, a successful real estate company in Centerville. Since I was an owner, Jane felt comfortable coming over to the office to have Nancy, our secretary, or I run Xerox copies for her. She would arrive with a large folder full of Blue Cross/Blue Shield papers, hospital receipts, doctors' bills, and prescriptions. If I saw her coming, I would sneak out the back door, leaving poor Nancy to deal with my mother. Jane would ask Nancy to make copies of every piece of paper. If it were a copy of a letter she was sending, she would have Nancy make a copy, then stop the machine while she folded the original, put it in an envelope, then seal it. Then she would hand Nancy another piece to be copied. When I was certain that Jane was gone, I would return to the office and try to slink past Nancy. I would have a very frustrated secretary to deal with, but Nancy's wrath was easier to deal with than my mother's demands at the copy machine. I did tell Jane that she could not expect Nancy to monopolize the copy machine because there were nearly forty people in the office who needed access to it.

"You are inconsiderate and ungrateful." She would say.

I never could figure out the ungrateful part. I felt that she was the one who should be grateful since Martha and I were picking up her rent, medical insurance, and car insurance.

Chapter Fourteen

Jane's Surgery

Jane had been living in Centerville for only about six months when her cardiologist determined that the doctors in Illinois were correct—Jane needed bypass surgery. She met with the surgeon who had the most experience, and he assured her that he could eliminate her chest pain and help her feel better over all. The surgery was scheduled for 8:00a.m., and we accompanied Jane to the hospital. She was placed in a room where the nurses would be doing pre-op preparations. The head nurse suggested that Martha and I go down to the cafeteria and have some coffee while they prepared Jane for surgery.

"Come back in about an hour," the nurse suggested.

We returned to Jane's room at the designated time and noticed that the nurses' moods had completely changed. One was in tears and the other two were noticeably upset.

"What's wrong?" We inquired.

"That woman is impossible," one nurse responded, clearly shaken.

As I inquired further, the nurse revealed that the young nurse that was crying had tried to insert an IV in Jane's arm and was having a hard time because Jane's veins were so small. At that point Jane chastised the nurse, calling her every name in the "book of incompetence" and accused her of being a nursing school dropout. The head nurse was also very upset because she could not convince Jane to sign the consent forms. The doctors were already waiting impatiently in surgery, angrily instructing the head nurse to do her job—they didn't have all day.

At this point, Jane said she was having second thoughts about having the surgery. "What should I do?" she asked me, probably wanting my reassurance.

I was not going to get caught in this "no win" trap. "The decision is completely yours. You have had opinions from two very fine doctors. They agree that open-heart surgery will help you. You have a capable surgeon waiting for you in the operating room. But I cannot make this decision for you."

Jane simply could not or would not make this decision. Minutes passed. Finally, a voice came over the intercom to Jane's room. It was the head surgeon calling to determine what the delay was. They were waiting in the operating room for the patient. We could hear the impatience in his voice, and the nurse was visibly upset. The nurse explained that the patient had not yet signed the consent form. There was no answer on the intercom. We waited for Jane to make her decision, embarrassed that she had come so far in her decision to have this surgery and was now backing down and being very unpleasant about the entire situation, her usual habit, I had regrettably come to realize.

We stepped out in to the hall with the nurse because there was no sense talking to Jane. We hoped that she would settle down and decide to sign the consent form. It wasn't long before we heard the clicking of wooden shoes in the hallway. It was the head surgeon, a Dutchman who was not in a very good mood. He grabbed the clipboard with the consent forms away from the nurse and headed into Jane's room. He slammed the door and within seconds we could hear both the doctor and Jane screaming at each other.

In a few minutes the doctor emerged from the room, handed the nurse the clipboard with the signed forms, saying, "She has signed the damned forms, now get her ass up to the OR before I change my mind!" He then turned to me and asked, "Are you her son?"

"Yes," I answered.

"If I do this surgery, I could extend her life by as much as ten or twelve years. You really should consider whether or not you want me to do this operation."

"It's her decision," I said.

I could not help but think, "welcome to my world." This is what it was like trying to deal with Jane for the last fifteen years or so.

I did find out from the nurse later that day that the screaming between Jane and the doctor started when Jane first spoke to the doctor.

"I probably do not need this operation," she said, then added, "you are just using me to get a new Mercedes."

The operation was a success. Jane was sent home in four days with a list of do's and don'ts. I do not believe she ever read the list. The doctors and nurses emphasized that she must quit smoking and start walking, but when Martha and I picked her up from the hospital, Jane wanted to stop at the first gas station to buy a pack of Camels.

"You haven't smoked for nearly a week, Jane. This would be a perfect time to stop."

Martha advised. "Besides, you're going to be prone to coughing anyway, and that won't be good for your incision. You need to take good care of yourself."

Jane was defiant and insisted that we stop nagging her. It seemed like she wanted to make herself miserable and in turn make our lives miserable.

Jane stayed at our house a couple of nights. She wanted to go on to her place. It was only six blocks away, so we felt that she would be fine. It would be more peaceful there without the hubbub of the kids. We could get groceries for her and check on her easily. The problem with Jane was that nothing we ever did satisfied her. We would bring dinner over to her, and it was something she didn't like or it had not been prepared to her liking. There was never a word of appreciation—not even a thank you.

In the weeks following her surgery, Jane's activities were very limited. She relied on Martha to take her to her frequent visits to her cardiologist, Dr. Marciukitis. According to Martha, she hated these office visits and would scowl when she walked into the doctor's office, complaining that she was not any better than she had been before her surgery. She was not a good patient and this frustrated the doctor. He knew that she had continued to smoke and this annoyed him. He was having a terrible time with Jane's blood pressure. After trying several combinations of medicines, he was not successful in getting it under control. Jane complained to him, insinuating that he was incompetent. I am sure he was not used to being chastised by one of his patients. I am also certain that she infuriated him with her constant griping. The doctor visits went on for months. Dr. Marciukitis became more frustrated with Jane and Jane became more vociferous in her complaints about him. We wanted to have faith in this doctor; he had a very good reputation, but months later, Jane didn't seem to improve very much. She seemed winded and tired all the time, and I began to wonder if the surgery really did work.

One day, I put a call in to Jane's doctor. I told him that I did not think Jane had improved since her surgery. The doctor explained that when they performed the surgery that they had improved the blood flow to her heart, but her heart was so damaged that it was not strong enough to pump the new supply of blood. I was shocked, and I immediately wondered why they didn't realize that before the surgery, and, if so, why had they performed the surgery. I never told Jane about my discussion with the cardiologist.

We all settled in to a routine. Jane would drive over to our house, sit at the kitchen table, smoke, and complain about the stupidity of the doctors, the lack of an interesting life, and how she missed Russ, her friend from Troy. They had become close friends and he had promised to come and visit her, but that promised visit was not coming to fruition. She would frequently call Russ, and they would have long phone conversations, but I am certain Russ's wife was not aware of the phone calls. Martha and I wondered what excuse Russ might use to get away from Troy to make a visit to Jane and how troubling such a visit would be if discovered by Russ's wife. Jane did not seem at all concerned about the feelings of Russ's wife.

Jane did not make any attempt to develop any kind of social life in Centerville. Her only real contacts were our family, the salespeople in my office, her hairdresser, her doctors, and her pharmacists. She did not seem interested in the boys' activities and since she could no longer take Shannon out in the car, she did not take much interest in her activities either She actually seemed to mellow a bit as the weeks and months passed. She didn't complain too much about the children and was noticeably less critical of us. Maybe she was just tired.

On a cold December Monday morning, our phone rang around 8:00 a.m. It was Jane.

"I think I'm having a heart attack," she stated.

"You need to hang up and dial 911 because I can't help you," I answered.

I sat down on the bed in our bedroom and opened the window. The fire station was right around the corner from Jane's place, and we could hear their sirens from our house if the windows were open.

Martha came in and asked, "Who called?"

"It was Jane."

"What does she want so early this morning?"

"She thinks she is having a heart attack. I told her to call 911 and I'm listening for the sirens." Just about that time, I heard the sirens start and stop, and I knew they were at Jane's.

"What are you going to do?" Martha asked.

"I plan to take a shower, get dressed, and go to the office. I have a sales meeting at 9:00."

"I'll go to the hospital and see what's going on," Martha said.

I told Martha to call me and keep me informed of the situation. I went to the office and Martha called to tell me that she was with Jane in the emergency room at Kettering Hospital. There had been no diagnosis of a heart attack, but her doctor had been called, and she and Jane were waiting for him to see her and give instructions as to her care and admission. Martha waited with Jane nearly six hours. Martha was impatient and insisted someone should make a decision about what was to be done with Jane. She was clearly very weak and having difficulty breathing. Finally, the emergency room nurse told Martha that she would have to take Jane home because her doctor was not going to admit her.

"Why not?" "He hasn't even been here to see her!"

The nurse told Martha that Dr. Marciukitis had been contacted, but told the nurses that he no longer wished to have Jane as a patient and would not be coming to see her. Martha knew that Jane had been a terrible patient and that she had infuriated Dr. Marciakitis with her incessant lamentations, but this was the first time Martha had ever heard of a doctor "firing" a patient. Yet, she knew there were a lot of "firsts" in Jane's history.

Martha knew that Jane was really sick this time. It was apparent that she was too weak to go to her apartment, and Martha felt that taking her to our house would not work. It was very hard to please her, and she really was very weak. She needed to be hospitalized. Martha called our family doctor and explained the situation to him.

"Take her to Saint Elizabeth's, Martha," Dr. Keyes said.

Martha loaded Jane in the car and took her to Saint E's. Dr. Keyes met Martha and Jane in the ER and quickly admitted her. She was placed in Intensive Care.

Martha called and told me of the situation, and I drove down to the hospital to see Jane. Jane was sleeping when I arrived, and hospital policy only allowed me to stay for a few minutes every three to four hours. Since she was resting comfortably, I went on home. I returned the next morning.

When I arrived in her room, Jane asked, "Where have you been?"

"They'll only let me stay a few minutes because you're in ICU." I answered.

I will never forget her response. "I'll bet you love that, don't you!"

I could only think to myself, "Here you are dying and you're still giving me shit!"

She seemed to improve that day and improved even more the following day. I told Martha that she would probably be moved out of intensive care soon. About 10:00 p.m. that evening, the hospital called to tell me that Jane had taken a turn for the worse, and that I should come down to the hospital. I had a bad feeling about the message and thought that Jane had probably passed away Our friends Chuck and Lonna had stopped over for a visit, so I asked Chuck to drive to the hospital with me, and Lonna said she would stay with Martha and the kids.

When Chuck and I arrived on Jane's floor, I asked him if he would wait in the waiting area while I checked on my mom. As I walked toward her room, I noticed that all of the breathing machines were in the hall, and I knew Jane was gone. When I got to the nurses' station, our doctor was there with a priest, and they informed me that Jane had died.

"Where is she?" I inquired.

They said that she was still in the room. I asked if I could go in and see her. They said that would be fine.

As I looked at her I felt no sorrow, just relief. It was as if a burden had been lifted from me. I was simply glad that all the years of problems had ended.

When Chuck and I drove back to the house, everyone wanted to know what had happened.

"How's Jane?" they asked.

I told them I had good news and bad news.

The kids said, "What is the bad news?"

I responded, "Your grandma died."

They then said, "What is the good news?"

"You can take all of her Christmas gifts back."

The kids did not ask any questions, nor did they display any sorrow. I told the kids to go on to bed, that there was nothing more to do tonight. I then called my friend George Miller who owned a funeral home and asked him to pick up Jane's body and have her cremated.

"Just let me know when the cremation is done, George." There is no need for a wake or a service. There is no one to mourn her."

"Well, John, I told you that someday I would tell you the whole story. I hope now you have a better understanding of why things happened the way they did."

Edwards Brothers Malloy
Thorofare, NJ USA
January 7, 2014